LIFE IN THE FAST LANE

Aidan Coles

PROMONTORY
P R E S S

LIFE IN THE FAST LANE

Copyright © 2013 by Aidan Coles

Promontory Press
www.promontorypress.com

First Edition: April 2013

ISBN 978-1-927559-07-9

Cover by CP Design.
Design and layout by SpicaBookDesign.

Printed in the United States

0 9 8 7 6 5 4 3 2 1

For my superheroes,
Mom and Dad

Table of Contents

Author's Note

NOTHING HAPPENS QUICKLY. Traffic moves slowly, time marches on. This book took years to evolve. I'd like to thank all my former coworkers and the dedicated police officers that spent time on the road with me. Thanks to Terry Humelstine and Bruce Campbell for instructing me in the Wreckmaster way. May we continue to grow in the vision that Donnie Cruse laid out and that his son Justin and his family continue on.

Most of all I'd like to thank my family and my best friend and partner, Sheila, for sticking by me through this long, strange trip.

I'd especially like to thank my brother Ben for giving me the opportunity that I would likely never have had otherwise.

To all the men and women in this industry, be proud of who you are and stand up as true professionals.

Foreword

IF SOCIETY COLLAPSED, who would you rather have with you? You have two choices.

The first choice is a military veteran trained in every kind of weapon, from pistols and assault rifles all the way up to naval guns and supersonic missiles. This veteran has served on five continents, speaks three languages and has a bachelor and masters degree. He has years of leadership experience, can organize resources and always keeps a cool head under pressure.

The second choice is a tow truck driver.

What's your choice?

Me, I'd take the second choice. Hands down.

If you'd like to know why, read this book. It's written by my older brother. I've spent years in wonder and admiration at his ability to weave his way in and out of shit, no matter how bad, and always emerge in one piece with those under his charge taken care of.

Tow truck driving is one of the most under-appreciated professions in our society, but towmen perform essential, often life-saving services day in and day out. They deserve a place of recognition right alongside police, firefighters and paramedics. Why? Read on.

I'm pretty sure there will never be a Towman's Calendar like their firefighting colleagues, nor a Gala Ball like the boys in blue (although either one would be pretty fun to see). Towmen are neither poster boys nor gentlemen, but our society would have a tough time without them.

And if society ever collapsed, I know exactly who I'd put my family under the care of: he drives a big truck that has a large hook on the back.

Bennett R. Coles, BA, MBA
Royal Canadian Navy (Retired)

LIFE IN THE FAST LANE

Playing In Traffic For a Living

EVERY SINGLE DAY, a tow truck operator is put in danger.

Vehicles have this really annoying habit of breaking down in inconvenient spots. Sure, some cars won't start in the driveway or in a parking stall at work. But when things go catastrophically wrong, it's usually at highway speeds in heavy traffic. If they have their wits about them, some drivers will try to coast to a relatively safe area, but on many highways there is no safe area when the shoulder is half a car width alongside the barricades. At least the occupants of the stricken car can stay belted in within their steel and fiberglass shell.

Sometimes the driver goes into shock and doesn't seem to realize where he is. When I arrive in my tow truck, the driver gets out and wanders around aimlessly as if we were parked in an empty field. I can't count how many times I've grabbed customers out of the path of oncoming traffic, or told them to just walk over to the shoulder and stay there. They want to help, or just watch that I don't scratch their Mercedes, but in doing so they become oblivious to their environment.

Anyone who works on the road – towmen,

phone repair crews, flag girls – doesn't call their reflective vest a safety vest: it's called a "Hit Me Vest". And those flashing yellow lights on top of the truck are apparently targets. They call to other drivers like a flame to a moth. Funny when you're in the car, but not so funny when you're standing on the roadside with cars passing within inches of you at over 100km per hour.

There's a new highway law known informally as "Slow Down, Move Over" that makes it illegal to travel at highway speed past any emergency vehicle on the road. So, let's make this clear, folks: tow trucks *are* emergency vehicles. Every year, tow truck drivers are killed or seriously injured because an inattentive driver hit them, the vehicle they were loading, or the tow truck.

Please remember, just because a towman is blocking your way, it doesn't mean he did it on purpose. We're just doing a job and trying to get traf-fic flowing as quickly as possible. Yelling at us, throwing coffee and insults, physically accosting us, or just leaning on your horn will not make us do our job any faster. In fact, it'll slow us down because now, we have to deal with your childish behaviour.

Also, if a tow truck is trying to cut across lanes with his beacons on, please don't block him. He's likely trying to get whatever is blocking your way, out of your way. But if you get the road rage thinking of 'I'm not letting anyone in' you're going to sit a very, very long time. If an ambulance, fire truck or police car did the same thing, you'd let them through without a second thought. If an accident is causing the delay, who's going to clear it?

That's right: the tow truck.

⋅⋗⋅

Curious to know what it's like at the pointy end of a tow operation? Let me tell you about one time I got a call to load a car on the Pat Bay Highway.

⋅⋗⋅

On this stretch of the highway, there was no shoulder to speak of; just a white line and a barricade five feet apart. The car in question was straddling the line with a blown front end: no chance it was going to move on its own power. Traffic was hurtling past us at 100km per hour as I hugged my truck into the barricade and backed as close to the car as I could with every emergency light I had on.

The customer was afraid to get out of the car. I couldn't blame her, so, from my cab, I signaled for her to roll down the passenger window and crawl out over the concrete to the relative safety of the grassy slope beyond the barricade.

With my truck in position, I assessed my options. Naturally, it was rush hour and traffic was heavy, both lanes of the highway full with frazzled, impatient commuters. There was no room to merge into the far lane and that steady stream of cars was whipping by within inches of the truck. I wasn't going into that, so I climbed out the passenger window and onto the deck. I was able to reach the controls from on top, fighting for balance on the deck as it angled downward. Operating heavy machinery takes concentration at all times, and now I was trying to manoeuver heavy hydraulics to grasp a 2000-pound car while teetering on an uneven platform. It was a scramble down the sloped deck to hook the chains onto the car and start to haul it up. I kept one eye close on my gear, the other on traffic. I didn't feel like dying that day.

Secured and ready to roll, I got my passenger in on the safe side, then slid around the light pylon onto the driver side step and squeezed in the door. Reasonably safe at last, I couldn't help but reflect on the fact that, not once, had any driver moved over to give me room, or slowed down.

But in those days, that's just the way it was. Nothing had gone wrong: no one had been hurt. Loaded and rolling, I took my customer and car to the yard, just another day in the life.

⋇

Fast-moving cars aren't always the biggest threat to a towman and you'd be surprised how diplomatic we occasionally have to be.

⋇

It was a hot, summer day and we got the call about 2:00pm to Dallas Road: scooter versus car.

This stretch of Dallas Road was beautiful and scenic, situated along the waterfront, so it was bustling with tourists and locals alike. Upon arrival at the crash site, I was informed that it was fatal and the road had to be shut down. Could I call a few more trucks for traffic control? I called it in and took up position, blocking the road at Cook Street a few blocks away.

Instantly, the abuse started.

"Get outta my way!!"

"You're just a tow truck. You can't block the road."

"Fucking asshole!"

"Got nothing better to do?"

Most people were frustrated because there wasn't an obvious detour route; others peppered me with questions about what had happened. At the start, I put on my best public servant face and told people politely that there was an accident and they'd have to go around, blah, blah, blah. But as the time wore on, I'll confess I started to get cranky under the barrage of abuse. It was 27 degrees and I was in jeans, work boots and uniform shirt. That was a dark blue shirt, by the way, offering no relief. My temper was growing shorter, especially with the idiots who thought they could drive past me.

At one point an officer – let's call him Waldo. You'll read more about him later – came down to check on me and give me an update, but he rode the surviving scooter down instead of a cruiser or cop bike. He parked the scooter behind my truck, out of view of the public. Just as he was parking, some guy pulled up and started in on me. I was standing in front of my truck, telling him to go around and, to be fair, I wasn't being all that polite anymore. After a heated exchange where my lineage and virility were both challenged, buddy decided he was going to drive through anyway. His lurching car banged against my leg, nearly taking me down.

The cop, Waldo, who'd stayed hiding behind my truck and listening to the whole exchange, stepped out in front of this idiot and forced him to stop. My man in blue walked over to the window and proceeded to ask why buddy thought that it was okay to drive through a roadblock, berate an emergency worker, endanger said worker and a whole host of bad things. He then took buddy's license, registration and keys and told him to get out and wait.

Since Waldo had ridden down on the scooter, he had no computer to access buddy's information. He could have easily just called his dispatch over the radio, but he had a better idea: he rode back up to the accident scene, grabbed some water and drove back down in his cruiser. He parked in front of me, blocking off the road completely, and sat in the car apparently working on the computer.

He motioned me over. "Get in." He handed me the water as I slid into the passenger seat. "You aren't getting the accident tow are you?"

I wasn't because they needed a deck and I was in a wrecker.

"How'd you like one?" he asked.

I looked at him quizzically.

He nodded toward the idiot driver. "Dumbass has a suspended licence."

We sat there for a little while in the air conditioned cruiser, playing solitaire on the computer while buddy got hotter and bitchier. I got out when required to reroute other people.

Finally, Waldo walked over to buddy sitting

on his car. When he started with the tickets, buddy was mad and swearing, but when he told him that I was towing his car because of a suspended licence and that he was losing it for thirty days, buddy was livid. I pulled my truck into position, while still blocking the road, started his car and drove it to the rear of my truck. I hooked it up and then used the whole unit as a complete road block.

Waldo sent him on his way, telling him he couldn't even walk through the accident scene and that he would have to circumnavigate the park.

I could hear buddy swearing for miles.

❧

There are a couple of important lessons that I hope buddy learned from that incident, aside from the obvious stuff, like don't drive with a suspended license or swear at police officers:

1. Towmen are people too and they have feelings: don't yell at them because it won't make the situation better.
2. When a tow truck is blocking the road and you're told to find another route, take it on faith that the towman isn't doing this just to piss you off: there's probably a very serious reason for the roadblock.
3. Towmen are emergency workers: treat them with the same respect you'd afford a firefighter or paramedic.
4. Towmen work with police every day: you probably won't get a sympathetic ear from a cop if you've been harassing a tow truck driver.

That fourth point is this: sometimes the only saving grace of my job – considering how often I'm working alone, in the dark, in the middle of no-where – whenever it comes down to my word against someone else's, it's good to have a reputation for professionalism.

For example, one time I was hooking up a car on the side of the Trans-Canada Highway at Thetis Lake. There wasn't much of a shoulder, but at least I could work completely off to the side of the main lanes of traffic. I was in an old wrecker and was about to hook up an old boat of a car. It was 2:00am, a cool summer night. There were no lights on that section of the highway and a long, sweeping corner stretched downhill toward me. I threw on the beacons and all rear lights to provide the highest visibility, knowing that most cars even at that time would be moving well above the 90km speed limit.

Despite the precautions, I was feeling apprehensive as I backed the truck into position. Some sixth sense told me to hug the side of the truck as I hopped out to hook up. I grabbed a J-hook out of the tool box and started toward the back of the truck.

Suddenly, a brilliant pair of lights appeared around the corner: a car coming down the highway. Keeping my eyes on that car, I bent down to place J-hook, holding the hook in my left hand and the chain in my right. I was just past my rear wheels when the car screamed down on me. He was close. Really close.

Pressed against the side of the truck, I had nowhere to go. His mirror clipped my hip and spun me up the side of the truck, knocking the J-hook and chain clear out of my hands. Through the agony of impact, I vaguely heard the sound of glass shattering.

The car slammed on the brakes and slid to a stop a few hundred metres away. The driver leapt out immediately, but his body language indicated that he was furious, not concerned. Pushing down the urge to vomit from the pain, I limped down the shoulder toward him, noting with some satisfaction that my J-hook had flown right through his back window. He inspected the damage with increasing anger, his words carrying up to where I'd now recovered the chain.

Ignoring his acid remarks, I grabbed my J-hook out of his back seat and turned to him. He still looked ready to lay into me about his window, but I think my expression alone silenced him. Either that, or the J-hook and chain I now hefted in my hands.

"You nearly killed me," I said with remarkable calm. "Right now, I feel like repaying the favour."

I took his licence plate and limped back to the truck to hook up. He drove away without even asking if I was okay.

I hooked up, got going and then called Dispatch to say I was heading to the cop shop after the tow. When I got to the police and filed a report, they told me buddy had already reported me as a distraction and that I was blocking the highway. I told the officer my version of the events and showed him the growing purple bruise on my hip. There wasn't a lot of grey area left in the story after that. I believe the driver was charged with undue care and attention, plus a note was put on his insurance file, so he had to pay for his back window.

In that case, I was lucky because I had a good relationship with the police and they knew me to be an honest guy who towed efficiently and without undue disruption to traffic. But it could have gone really differently: before the "Slow Down, Move Over" law was passed, I had nothing with which to defend myself in a no-witness situation like that.

⋇

As in any profession, a reputation is built up over years of good work. I've enjoyed the support of most local police because we work together so much, but every now and then I find myself having to deal with different sorts of officials who don't know me. That wouldn't be so bad, except for the fact that, sometimes, these folks arrive with pre-conceived notions of what a tow truck driver is good for.

⋇

The most dramatic example I can remember began, as these things so often do, with sirens. Even though I was sitting at home, all I could hear was sirens. The pager went off and I called in.

Major crash on the bridge. Go check it out and see what's needed.

I started rolling, but didn't even make it a kilometer before bumper-to-bumper traffic blocked the road. I threw on the beacons and cruised slowly down the oncoming lane. The Sooke bridge was on the other side of our small town and it was the only way in and out. As I approached, I could see that it was a madhouse: police, fire and ambulances everywhere. I was waved through the barricade and finally got the chance to assess the situation.

The road before me was dominated by a crashed 4x4 leaning heavily where a wheel was torn clear off. Just beyond, was a mangled car where firemen were using the jaws to get someone out. But neither of those vehicles were the real problem.

On the edge of the bridge, balanced precariously over the main span supports, was a tractor trailer. The flat deck trailer still had its rear wheels on the bridge deck, the full load of steel weighing it down enough to barely counteract the pull of the tractor that hung freely over the side of the bridge, somehow still connected to its load.

The volunteer fire department had hooked a winch from their rescue truck to the nose of the tractor to stabilize the front end. The wreck was clearly unstable, though, so I quickly positioned my truck out of the way of the firemen and away from any skid marks the cops would want to investigate later. I scrambled to get two lines from my truck hooked on to the rear of the trailer to stabilize. It worked and we all breathed a sigh of relief.

And then we sat, trying to keep things still. The tractor dangled over the river; the flat deck trailer remained pinned by its shaken load of steel.

All the bigwigs were arriving now: the police chief, fire chief and even the mayor. I told them we were looking at least an 11-hour delay, maybe 12. Based on their stupefied reactions, you'd think I'd told them that aliens were forbidding us to move.

All three of them had one priority: get the traffic rolling across the bridge again. I stated flatly that this was impossible with all the equipment at present. But I guess these three small town officials must have run a civil engineering shop or something before running for office, since they over-ruled me with such certainty.

Thankfully, as I made my last defence of the laws of physics, an engineer from the Department of Roads arrived. He told the mayor and her goons that, before the public was allowed on the bridge, a structural engineer had to assess the damage. That ban even included recovery operations, which meant we couldn't even call for heavy equipment to pull the tractor trailer out of the way. It also seemed prudent at that time to remind the bigwigs, especially the police chief, that no recovery operation could happen until the RCMP Crash Analysis Team had done their work.

By now, traffic was backing up horribly. Did I mention that this bridge was the only way in or out of Sooke as well as all the towns west of it? Twelve thousand people commuted into Victoria every day over this bridge. Now, it was three o'clock and students from the high school on one side of the bridge were trying to get home.

Parents from the other side were trying to pick up children. And anyone who has worked on the road in any capacity knows that soccer moms on a mission are *nasty*.

The public was bitching and yelling at the mayor, who responded by storming around and barking orders at the emergency crews like she knew what she was doing, and failing miserably. She was clearly out of her depth, but instead of listening to the professionals, she fell back on the tried and tested leadership method of shouting.

The RCMP Crash Analysis Team arrived from Nanaimo within two hours, which was quite impressive considering the traffic mess on all roads leading to Sooke. They conducted their investigation while the fire crew continued to drain the fuel tanks on the tractor. The requested structural engineer arrived to assess the condition of the bridge span and he gave the okay for recovery operations once the RCMP team was done.

By now I'd had some time to put my brain to the problem: how do you recover a tractor trailer loaded with steel that was hanging half over a bridge? I'd been making phone calls. A 20-ton crane was trapped on the Sooke side of the bridge and I asked if he was available to assist; he said yes. The owner of the distressed rig had slowly been making his way out to us from Victoria with a 40-ton crane and trailer. I had our deck truck come and collect the two smaller, wrecked cars blocking the approach to the bridge while I stayed with the medium duty wrecker hooked as stabilization. I placed a call for a tandem wrecker from Victoria to recover and tow the tractor trailer once we'd cleared it.

While waiting for the RCMP and the engineer to finish their work, I presented my recovery plan to the two crane operators, the fire chief and police chief. We needed the whole bridge to remain shut down for us to work as there would be nearly one million pounds of equipment within a 400 yard area.

The bigwigs told me to wait for the tandem driver to present his plan since I was just some towing ape from Sooke. By now, I knew which big city driver was coming with the tandem and I knew he was one of the best and highest qualified drivers in the area. In fact, we'd done most of our provincial qualifications together.

When he arrived, all of the wigs swarmed him as he assessed the situation. He stopped them short, called me over and asked my opinion. I told him my plan. He agreed without issuing a single change. The two crane operators, fire chief and police chief all stopped and looked at me.

"He's more qualified than I am," said the tandem driver. "He knows what he's doing: you should listen to him."

I graciously deferred and commended the fire chief and police chief on their outstanding leadership throughout. Oh, fuck that! I stood there with the smuggest expression since 1976 when my little brother took the blame for my goofing around after bedtime.

Finally enjoying the full attention of the assembled operators, I gave directions to start moving the cranes and tow trucks into position. When we were ready, the slack was taken out of the lines and the two cranes began to lift in tandem. The tractor began to inch upward, away from the rushing water below. Then, a shudder and crack. I looked up and saw the jib of the 20-ton crane bend at a horrible angle.

I ran over to where he was climbing out of his cab. "I thought you said your crane could lift this."

He averted his eyes and started to unhook.

Now, we were down a crane and the traffic was probably backed up to nearly the Alberta border. We considered our remaining assets and came up with a slight change of plan. We used the 40-ton crane as a dead man as well as a lifting unit. Then the tractor and trailer were swung as a unit using the tandem tow tuck with two lines, my medium duty with two lines, and a whole lot of yelling back and forth.

As we had to have all the units tight together, the opposing lane was partially open, but we'd requested it stay closed until we had the truck on deck. It seemed, however, that our recommendations and experience meant nothing when Johnny Q Public needed to get home. So, the police chief ordered his boys to start letting cars through.

Right when the tractor trailer was midair.

I would have yelled for the cops to close off the bridge again, but I was way too busy trying to keep control of an airborne, steel-laden flat deck. We couldn't stop, so all we could do was complete the operation, pray the bridge held under the weight, and that nothing else snapped or toppled.

Finally, after a lot of delicate line movement, the tractor and trailer landed on the deck. There were no cheers, no applause. Just angry commuters fuming at us as they rolled past. Hungry, dehydrated, soaked in sweat and doubtless sporting some new grey hairs, I turned my attention to how we were going to get the wreck off the bridge for good. The front of the tractor was mangled horribly and it took some inventive hooking up to get it loaded. The drive shafts were pulled and it rolled off the bridge behind our heavy duty truck. The cranes were packed up; I retrieved all of my appropriate file numbers and, finally, the bridge was free to let traffic flow.

I'd been on the accident scene for 10 hours and 57 minutes. I looked at the mayor, glanced at my watch, then looked back at her. "Hmm. Three minutes early. You're welcome."

Her expression didn't mirror my wry amusement. But then, who really ever smiles at a tow truck driver?

Cat and Mouse

IT'S NO FUN to have your car towed. Whether voluntary or involuntary, nobody's impressed when facing a towman. When an involuntary situation arises – in other words, when your car's being towed against your will – it's akin to personal violation for some people.

"You have no right," is how the conversation usually starts.

For me as a towman, keeping a calm, professional demeanor is key. I've known some drivers who go itching for a fight, who aggravate people just for fun. I've also known arrogant dispatchers who think that every customer coming in is a total piece of shit, not worth the time to treat properly. They're wrong. Every customer deserves to be treated with respect.

On the flip side, every customer who comes in yelling and screaming deserves a CLOSED sign until they can treat the employees with the same respect. So many customers come in yelling because they see that behaviour on TV and think that's the way to deal with towmen. They couldn't be further from the truth.

Reality TV is so far from reality that it's laughable. Most of those shows are staged and many of the participants purposefully wind up unsuspecting customers into a rage just for the camera. In reality, the viewing audience would see a calm, relaxed atmosphere where, only occasionally, would they see a total retard. But that doesn't make good TV now, does it? If you're ever in a situation where you need to deal with a towman, stay calm. It works wonders.

❧

Take, for example, the time I was dispatched to tow an illegally-parked vehicle downtown. I found the offender and saw that it was a big, old, red Ford pickup. I decided quickly to tow it from the front, then backed up into position. I engaged the PTO, jumped down, dropped the sling right under the front bumper and threw a J-hook under the driver's side, quickly hooking to sling. I needed only a few more seconds to get to other side and finish.

"Hey Fucker! That's my truck!" A young, burly construction guy charged toward me.

I looked him calmly in the eye. "Sir, you're being towed for city tickets. Would you please hand over the keys?"

He pushed past me and jumped into his truck. "Fuck you!"

I hooked up the other J-hook quickly, then reached for the controls. The pickup engine roared to life. I jammed my control lever and lifted the pickup skyward until the front tires were two feet off the ground. Buddy was still determined to move the truck on the sling, creating a dangerous situation for himself, me and all other people and vehicles in the area.

Gritting my teeth, I walked around to the driver's door of his vehicle, opened it, reached in and yanked the keys out of the ignition. (Thankfully, those old Fords have their ignition on the far left lower portion on the dash.) So now I had his keys *and* his truck. The new problem facing me, though, was that I now had a big, angry, trapped construction worker as well.

Thankfully, since I hadn't answered the radio for some time, our nearby service van stopped by just then to check on me. I was trying to talk this guy out of his truck while he hurled abuse at me, clearly looking for a fight. But the bastard wouldn't get out of the pickup. And that's all I wanted.

When Steve showed up in the service van, I saw an opportunity.

I grabbed buddy by the shirt and hauled him out, threw his pickup in neutral and ran for my idling truck. I jumped in and put my foot to the floor. Buddy was immediately distracted by Steve, who started taunting him mercilessly from the service van. Once I was moving and clear, Steve hammered the gas and drove away from a dumbfounded and now hopping-mad owner.

"You good?" came Steve's voice over the radio.

"Yeah, thanks dude," I said, still gasping for air. "You arrived in perfect timing. And thanks for being your usual asshole self to distract him."

"No problem," Steve laughed. "See you at the yard."

So we got the truck after all, and buddy deserved his humiliation for parking illegally so many times and then trying to interfere with our police-appointed duty. Being rude and aggressive with me didn't win him anything but an uncooperative dispatch when he finally slunk in to pay his fees and get his pickup.

🍵

Now compare that experience to this one: there was this one van we used to tow all the time for parking illegally. She was a young lady, working several jobs in the downtown core, trying to scrape by. We used to get her every month from two or three areas around her work. At first, she parked where she could see her van and quickly figured out which were the hardest spots for us to get at. That would give her enough time to see us, come running out into the street to bombard us with screaming or crying or whatever. But then, after the third or fourth time I got her, she changed.

She walked up to me quite calmly. "Hi. Same place still?"

I stopped what I was doing and turned to face her. She was holding the keys out towards me with a coffee and a smile. Slightly dumbfounded, I smiled back. "Giving up so easy this time?"

Laughing, she replied. "You guys have gotten my van every time without fail for six months. I should just leave it unlocked with the keys in it. I see how hard you work and realize I've put you through hell. Maybe I should actually say thanks for the effort." She offered the coffee and keys again.

I took the keys, thought about it for a minute, then accepted the coffee.

"Take care of my baby," she said as she turned away. "I'll pick her up after work."

I finished hooking up and called it in. She played cat and mouse with us in the same block over the next year. But every time we hooked her van, she came out with keys and coffee for whichever driver happened to get her. No issue, just a smile. She knew she was busted and figured that every month the admin fee and towing was actually cheaper than parking downtown. Plus, she knew it was safe and secure in our compound and didn't worry about anyone breaking into it or stealing it.

⋇

Since we're on the subject, let's talk about tickets. City tickets always present interesting situations. The City will tow a vehicle and hold it until parking fines and towing fees are paid. However, it becomes quite a game of cat and mouse, treachery and deceit, an all-out who gets who first. The rules of the game are quite simple, but rarely are they followed by both participants:

1. Pay for your parking.
2. If you choose not to pay, you will receive a ticket with a set fine.
3. If you receive a ticket, please pay it promptly.
4. Should you choose not to pay, it goes against the license plate of vehicle.
5. If you continue to park illegally, receive tickets and refuse to pay, your license plate goes on a "hit list" with the Commissionaires.
6. Should you receive 3 or more tickets that you

ignore for more than 3 months, your car is liable for towing.

7. If things progress to this point, at any time your vehicle is parked in a city parking stall or on a city street, you are subject to tow.

Now the fun starts. To be towed, a number of things have to happen:

8. Commissionaire calls the City office that tracks vehicles with outstanding tickets.
9. Commissionaire is informed it is subject to tow and confirmed through the database.
10. Commissionaire requests a tow truck and gives the pertinent information.
11. Towing company is called and provided with offending vehicle's location, make, model, color and license number.
12. Tow truck is dispatched to find offending vehicle.
13. Upon locating said vehicle, tow operator calls dispatch and informs that they are attempting to hook.
14. Tow dispatch calls commissionaire dispatch to inform that tow operator is attempting to hook said vehicle and asks if it is approved to tow.
15. Commissionaire dispatch reconfirms that said vehicle is subject to tow and has not paid fines through the database. They relay that information to tow dispatch and gives "Go Ahead to Tow" authorization.
16. As soon as tow operator is hooked, he must

call for confirmation to remove vehicle and cannot move until receiving authorization.

17. Tow dispatch gives authorization to tow based on Commissionaire authorization.

18. Tow operator then completes hook up and tows vehicle to compound.

At this point, the vehicle owner enters the game.

19. Vehicle owner realizes his/her vehicle is gone and contacts City Hall.

20. Vehicle owner must *first* attend City Hall and pay $200 in "administrative fees" *plus* make arrangements to pay, or pay off, outstanding fines before going to tow compound to collect vehicle.

21. Once vehicle owner has a receipt of payment of administrative fee they may go to tow compound and collect vehicle *after* paying tow fees.

22. Only after all fees are paid, proper ID is shown and confirmation that person picking up vehicle is the Registered Owner of said vehicle is vehicle released to vehicle owner or designated representative.

It is a very involved process, with a great deal of redundancy to protect the ve-hicle owner against an unauthorized tow away. It also takes a few minutes to get said authorization with busy phone lines, etc.

So hopefully you can see, having read the very

involved and time consuming process involved in towing a car, that that owners very often will arrive mid-hook. Some are upset, some are angry, some are downright enraged and some fully accept that, "Ha ha. You got me".

As I've said before, the act of towing a person's vehicle amounts to a personal violation to some people and they react as one would expect to that – like buddy the construction worker. Other people realize that they are in the wrong and react like poorly-behaved children caught with their hand in the cookie jar – that's most folks. My personal favorites, though, are the repeat offenders who know full well what the deal is, yet continue to play the game and simply try to get away with whatever they can – like our friend the waitress. Then, there are the really weird situations.

꙳

I was in the deck truck and ordered on a City Tickets call. The previous deck driver would refuse city tickets because, trying to snatch a vehicle with a 30-foot truck can get quite interesting and blocking entire streets can cause a lot of issues. But he wasn't very experienced and didn't know many tricks of the trade. I, on the other hand, had been stealing cars legally with a deck truck for many years and knew several tricks to expedite a tough, tight load. Once I received the information, I set off on the hunt.

I found the offending vehicle parked on a yellow line right at the end of a side street that opened to a busy intersection. In order to get to this one, I'd have to block the intersection for a minute, using beacons which attract far too much unwanted attention.

I called in, "Going for a hook," and lined up.

I backed up to within inches of the offending vehicle, hopped out and began to drop my deck. The deck scooped under the front wheels and I slid under to attach the bridle. As I was pulling the cable tight, this guy ran over and jumped up on my truck, trying to kick the cable out. I jammed it as tight as a piano wire. Now he's yelling and swearing. He kicked the skates out of my hand and got right in my face, trying to shove me off the controls. I told him that he was being towed for city tickets, etc: go away or give me the keys.

This guy was tall, skinny, covered in tattoos and obviously trying to get me to hit him. He kept saying things like, "Do you know who I am?"

My response was simple. "I don't give a fuck who you are, I'm taking the car. You have no idea who I am."

Throughout this interaction, there was some other asshole in a nearby car yelling at us, telling tattoo-man that it's illegal; just hit the tower, I got your back, etc. Plus, there was a lady looking at me, asking if I'm okay and do I need police? I just nodded at her, shoved buddy off me and reached for my radio.

"Get the cops here now!" I yelled into my radio. As I turned back, tattoo-man tried to push me into the side of the truck.

At that point, a young lady stormed out of the salon, saying it's her car. I asked tattoo-man who the registered owner was, but he still kept at me.

Now they were both in my face, with the asshole in car still egging them on, and I was starting to vibrate with adrenaline, barely able to keep my cool.

Sirens in the distance! The cavalry! Tattoo-man heard them and disappeared back into the salon. Salon-girl stayed, though, yelling until the first police car arrived. Then another and another.

We were separated and I was asked what happened. I told the older officer – good ol' Waldo – that tattoo-man was lucky I didn't take him out.

Waldo looked at me. "No shit, I've seen what you can do to idiots. What do you want me to do?"

"Just let him know how close he came to having his face bounced off my truck and that he should be really careful where he tries to pull his macho shit."

The other cop listened to salon-girl's side of the sob story and informed her that, yes, I had every legal right to tow her car and that she can pick it up at the compound *after* dealing with City Hall. Then he told her to go away and let me finish my job.

Waldo went in and read the riot act to tattoo-man in front everyone, then held him for over an hour while he ran his record and, basically, gave him the gears.

Turned out, tattoo-man wasn't the owner, the boyfriend or even a friend. He was just some wannabe trying to impress the cute girl who owned the car.

A Cop Named Waldo

I'M HAPPY TO SAY that I've enjoyed a good relationship with the police throughout my professional life. This is good despite the fact that, being on the bad side of cops is no fun, but it's also allowed me to see their human side. They get beat on by the public almost as much as towmen do, so maybe it's that mutual sense of appreciation that urges both groups to have a lot of fun. Often at each other's expense.

There was one particular officer who loved to play practical jokes. I'll call him Waldo to protect his identity. He was the kind of guy who'd call our line with a horrendous foreign accent and drive the poor dispatch mental. Or, he'd steal our trucks. Yeah, you read that right: a cop who stole tow trucks. Never for long and never for keeps, but still. It was only a matter of time before we overcame our respect for the uniform and decided to get back at him.

❧

On one snowy morning, Waldo pulled into the driveway of our yard in his cruiser and left it blocking the garage. This was his usual spot – not specifically in the way of our regular activities, but irritating enough.

It had been snowing for the last few days and there was about a foot of the stuff in the stalls next to his cruiser. One of our guys took him out back to check out a possible stolen vehicle. His partner was in on the gag and went along to slow the inspection down.

We didn't waste a second. With shovels, boards and bare hands, five of us heaped snow onto Waldo's cruiser, bringing down a man-made blizzard like Victoria had never seen. We buried the car right up to the roof line, ensuring all four doors were hidden inside a three-foot thick tomb of snow. It took only about four minutes, but each one of us wasted precious seconds looking back at the lot, just in case our victim had caught wind of trouble.

Task complete, I walked out back and, trying to hide my heavy breathing, asked Waldo's partner to help me inside while Waldo continued the search of the stolen vehicle. Once inside, Waldo's partner called the station and asked for a fake emergency call to be sent to him and Waldo: a Code 4. He had his own cruiser and he'd parked out on the street. Then he walked back outside.

As we huddled inside the open door, stifling the occasional giggle, we heard the police radios crackle to life: Code 4, major emergency, go now, full lights and sirens!

Both cops took off running for the front gate of the yard. We dashed through the maintenance bay and plastered ourselves against the windows inside Dispatch's office, waiting for the fun.

Waldo's partner was out in a flash, jumping

in his cruiser and peeling out. Waldo charged through the gate... and stopped dead. Then, he simply stood and stared. We'd locked the garage door, the front door and nobody was out on the street. We'd even moved all the trucks, so no shovels were close by. But we had left a child's beach shovel sitting on top of the pile.

He was stunned and flustered, but give credit to that keen police mind: he quickly realized what was going on. He called his station to calmly inform them he would not be able to respond to the Code 4. We kept the doors locked and let him dig his way into the cruiser. By the time he got in he was cold, wet and grumpy, but grudgingly laughing too. He knew he'd been caught and he could appreciate the infantile genius of our gag.

꩜

Things cooled off in the practical joke war for a while, but only a few months went by before the mad foreigners started calling Dispatch and trucks started taking themselves for drives again. By now, it was early summer and Waldo was parking in his usual spot. He left the cruiser running with the air conditioning on – to keep the computer cool, he claimed – but he knew better than to trust any of us, so he locked the doors with his spare key. He thought he was smart, but we'd been scheming, and waiting for such a opportunity.

This being a tow yard and all, we had a lot of broken window glass from all the crashes we recovered. While Waldo was out back, one of us (might have been me) unlocked his car – as towmen are rather skilled at doing – and rolled down all four windows while the rest of us spread broken glass across the floor and seats. We left the car running to keep the computer cool.

When he emerged a few minutes later, his jaw dropped in horror. Although our yard was not in a nice part of town, he didn't expect to be vandalized. The jackals, howling with laughter inside the shop, told him something was up, but he still didn't cotton on. By the time he came inside most of my buddies had vanished like ninjas, but I stayed and handed him a bucket and broom. He snatched it out of my hands and stormed outside, still not sure how he was going to explain this one. Somebody behind the door told him that he should lift his windows to make sure he got all the glass. Then the gig was up.

As we all helped him sweep the glass out of his car, he again commended us on our childish cunning.

❦

Another time, Waldo stopped by the yard to get some parts for his personal truck. His truck wouldn't start – which we had nothing to do with, just to put that on record in case he ever reads this book – and he was going to be late for work.

I told him to leave his truck at our yard until after his shift and that I'd give him a ride to work. Again, I feel the necessity to portray my innocence in the affairs of that day; I couldn't possibly have been involved in the tomfoolery that followed.

Apparently, as soon as we left, our owner and her sister ran to Staples to buy all the pink Post It notes in stock. I'm talking thousands of them. When they returned, they started to plaster them on Waldo's white truck. Eventually, I made it back to the yard and saw the site of the truck slowly changing colour. Each driver was asked to help in the effort, but everyone of us declined: we knew the retribution would be severe and most of us were already under threat from past, unforgiven pranks. Something about snow and windows?

The girls spent hours covering his truck in those pink Post It notes, but they weren't content to leave it at that. Somehow they'd gotten their hands on blue Post It notes too, and in the centre of his hood, they created an outline of a giant, blue penis.

When he returned from his shift, there proudly stood his truck, all decked out in pink and blue. Naturally, we were all hunkered inside Dispatch's office, anticipating his reaction, but even we were surprised at the roar of laughter that echoed across the street. He thought it was hilarious and laughed for a long time, then drove it home looking like that. In fact, he left it that way until it rained the next day and his white pickup took on the colour of the Post It notes. At least it matched the trail of pink Post It notes from our yard, onto the highway, through the subdivision to his house.

✿

The pranks finally came to an end in a very unusual way, with an incident that wasn't meant as a prank at all. Two of us were called to Burnside and Harriet for a two-car crash. I arrived in my wrecker and my partner in his. Waldo and his partner had blocked the lanes with their cop Harleys and gave us the go ahead to clear the scene. It was rush hour and traffic was backing up fast. My partner and I loaded our vehicles and pulled off into a parking lot on the corner.

Waldo was talking to the victims and doing his paper work while his partner directed traffic around us. As soon as we'd finished sweeping and the road was clear, Waldo's partner pulled his bike into the parking lot. We were waiting for Waldo to move his bike. And waiting. And waiting. Traffic was really backing up around it.

Since I'd ridden the police bikes before and had essentially been given free rein to move police equipment in the past, I thought nothing of walking over to the Harley, hopping on, starting it up and driving it into the parking lot. As I pulled up to Waldo, he was seething. I honestly thought his helmet was going to burst off his head. "Don't. Ever. Do that again."

I knew he was mad, so I quickly got off the bike, skulked over to his partner and asked what I'd done wrong. I honestly didn't see a problem, but was quickly corrected.

"You had no helmet," Waldo's partner explained, "no vest and no police uniform on. And you did it front of a full intersection of the public. I suggest you just go get that wreck to the yard and I'll cover your escape."

I knew he was serious and figured that I'd

committed a major faux pas, so I hightailed it out of there.

The next day, Waldo came to the yard and found me. He'd cooled off, but was still pretty pissed. I told him I was sorry and gave my excuses. He smiled and agreed with his partner's assessment, but told me that, hearing his bike start up and drive away was what got him the most: he'd actually thought someone was stealing it. To this day, I haven't tried to steal his bike again. Not that I was actually trying to steal it.

I guess we all have to grow up eventually, and when Waldo got promoted within the police force he seemed to realize that all those pranks, as much as they'd brightened our days, had to stop.

The Good

TOWMEN ARE HUMAN. There, I said it. True, we sometimes come across as big, mean hooligans that have nothing better to do than to steal a car, or we look like some badass biker that you'd be scared to let your wife get in the truck with. Many of us have been trying to get away from the stereotypical image over the years but, let's face it, we are who we are.

≫

Take, for example, the time I was working at a small towing company with a good buddy of mine named Rob. Things were very slow and money was tight. Everyone was edgy about pay and whether we would survive the season. The boss, in particular, was always on edge and he looked for any reason to pick on us just to blow off some of the steam he understandably had.

It had been going on for weeks and was happening earlier and earlier each day. Soon enough, the abuse started the moment we walked in the door to begin our shift at 6:30 am. We hadn't even opened our coffees and we were getting shit on. Rob and I had had enough. That day we argued with the boss and told him to back off and leave us alone. We understood his frustration but we were not targets, especially at 6:30! We all came to the agreement that he would make sure to leave us alone until we'd finished our first coffee.

So, I went out that day and bought the biggest travel mug I could find: it was a two-litre monster, more than I could really drink, but I made my point. I was set.

When I walked in the next morning, carrying my giant cup, he just smiled at my audacity and said, "Okay, I promised."

Moments later, Rob walked in holding a travel mug he'd had in his closet that he had bought on his last trip to the States. It was a full gallon mug, as big as his head!

As he sat down, Rob saw my cup and winked at me, then looked at the boss. "I should be good for the day, eh?"

From then on, the boss left us alone until we'd finished our first cup, regardless of size.

⊕

In general, I'd like to say that, underneath all that grime, towmen are a bunch of big, cuddly teddy bears, but I'd be lying. Not to say we aren't a fun bunch of folks; that side of us is just usually hidden from the general public. As a yard manager, I could usually gauge the productivity of my team by the amount of practical jokes going on, although the degree of damage caused was something I had to watch. When the jokes were harmless I tolerated them, as they were good for morale and useful work was still being done. But when the joke started to involve destruction of property, I knew that more chores needed to be handed out.

⋆

It had been a crappy summer so far: rain, overcast and cold. But today, oh, today was different. Dawn broke clear and bright. The day shift team trundled in at the usual 7:00 to 7:25ish, and the night crew trundled off after the usual banter and cajoling. All sixteen of us on the day shift sat around drinking coffee, smoking cigarettes, eating breakfast, or doing some combination thereof. It had been a quiet few days and we knew most of the traffic cops were off on a course, so it was likely today was going to be more of the same. All the trucks were warmed up and a few guys went off to do patrols and carry on with the day.

By 10:00 no calls had come in and everyone was starting to get a little antsy in the pantsy. It's been said that idle hands are the devil's playthings. Well, you've never seen sixteen bored tow truck operators cooped up in a tiny office. The minor hijinks were steadily growing in violence until Dispatch yelled at everyone to get out.

We all moped around outside, looking for something to do. This was never a good situation, especially with the nearby preponderance of scrap cars, scooters and, especially, highly flammable and explosive chemicals. All the possible productive work that could've been done had been done earlier in the week: there was no maintenance, no cleaning, not even the scrapping of cars to do.

Then, someone found a football in the back of a truck. Oh, joy, oh bliss! We started passing it back and forth, then running with it. Quickly, it became a scrum match. Because we had shunted cars earlier on in the week, we had an entire section of the yard cleared of cars, now parked in beautifully-defined and painted stalls: the perfect football field, nearly sixty yards long and thirty feet wide. The ideal size for out-of-shape, overweight, smoking, McDonald's-eating, steel toe-wearing hooligans needing to blow off some steam.

We played on and on into the day, any occasional call taken by whoever was up next and someone rotated in. We used our reflective vests as flags instead of tackling on the asphalt, but a number of aggressive flag pulls ended up in a couple of guys sliding across the pavement. Each guy grabbed water and food as they went out on calls and waited patiently (sort of) to get back in the game. By the end of the day the score was somewhere in the area of 400 to 401, but since there was a constant rotation of players changing sides three or four times throughout the day, nobody was a winner or loser. We all stank of sweat, were filthy from rolling on the dusty pavement, and a few guys had open road rash wounds. But we were happy, tired and completely satisfied.

When the night shift rolled in, they saw 16 guys slouching around in exhaustion.

"Busy day? You guys look like you ran your asses off."

We all kind of smiled and just nodded. In my

opinion, it was probably one of the best days I spent with that crew in the five years we worked together. And best of all for the bosses, nothing got blown up.

ॐ

Now I'm not saying that we ever tried to blow anything up, but sometimes we did engage in stress-testing of equipment. Quite often, we have vehicles left unclaimed. Most end up going to scrap and crushed, some get resold and the odd few get turned into race cars. That particular summer we had five scooters brought in which had been stolen and then recovered. They were all from a local rental company and since the company had been paid out by their insurance and the scooters weren't in serviceable condition for rentals, they had been left with us. We used them to go to the far end of the lot to retrieve info from cars, check locations in parking stalls and just fool around when bored.

One Saturday evening during the summer we were all in to cover police roadblocks, but it was a slow night and none of us had been called out. A few of us had been racing each other on the scooters from the far end of the lot, taking the end corner at high speed, then gunning it for the front of the compound, stopping before hitting the gate or office.

Then someone found a sheet of plywood and some 2x4s. A makeshift ramp was assembled and we took turns jumping the scooters. Keep in mind, these are 50cc scooters and most of us were 200lb plus, so control and speed did not go hand in hand. We were running them at full throttle, scraping pegs on the corner and there were some spectacular wipeouts.

As the evening wore on, the speeds increased and so did the jump height. Two of the scooters fell victim to heavy weight and high speed crashing down onto the pavement: the first snapped a set of front forks clear off on impact, while the second dropped in half while exploding the rear tire. But we kept on going. Friends had come by and there was a large cheering squad for each attempt.

On one attempt, my buddy Steve landed badly and jumped clear of the now out-of-control scooter. He executed a perfect running-leaping-half-twist-triple-gainer as the now-unmanned scooter rocketed out the gate at high speed. We all turned to watch as it careened towards a brand new tow truck. It glanced off the front bumper and bounced end over end into the building across the alley. There were gasps, laughs and then a collective scamper to collect the pieces before anyone saw.

By the end of the night, we were hitting 80km per hour through the corner and clearing three feet high at the apex of our 20-foot jumps. To their credit, the last two scooters took everything we threw at them and kept on going. We finally gave up at around 1:00am when they ran out of gas.

The following Monday morning, a memo was posted about noise complaints from the neighboring bar and that we were to cease and desist with anymore "rally racing, stunting or general mayhem". Supposedly, the cops on shift had been patrolling the area and could hear us from blocks away while dealing with drunks in front of a bar, then had periodically watched our antics from the overhead parking lot. I guess we were a little more vocal than we'd thought.

⚡

I know I said that we never actually tried to blow anything up. Okay, so maybe I lied. As most people know, Halloween is for trick or treating, people in costume, general tomfoolery, fireworks, minor vandalism, public drunkenness; a time when people can let their inner evil, mischievous, devil-may-care attitude come out.

This particular Halloween had been a quiet one and, as usual, we were bored and looking for mischief. The last of our battle-hardened scooters had been sent to scrap, but one of the guys had brought small firecrackers in. We were setting them off and giggling like school girls when one of us – might've been me – suggested making a more dynamic bang.

We scrounged the lot and the back shop, coming up with pop cans, tennis balls and pop bottles. We stood at the mechanics bench and rooted around for any and all flammable substances, and maybe a few toxic chemicals. We started mixing and matching in the cans, tennis balls and pop bottles to see what kind of big bang we could make.

Unintentionally, we created an explosive form of napalm. It was loud, concussive and left divots in the pavement while creating a bright flash. We were having a great time. Dispatch was hiding in her office and refused to come out since we were blowing these bombs up in the driveway in front of her window. Two or three times, the police drove by slowly, spotlights on, only to find the whole crew standing on the curb, smiling like a bunch of 200-lb cherubs.

Then, someone – might've been me – suggested that we add oxy-acetylene to the mix. None of the other guys had ever done this before, so it was a new way to create our big bang. The basic concept is simple: take a two-litre plastic pop bottle, fill it with a 2:1 mixture of oxygen and acetylene from welding torches, add a paper fuse, light and run away.

The resulting bang was extremely loud, concussive and bright but, other than plastic shrapnel, completely harmless. After a bit of trial and error, we figured out the best mixture. Then we decided to use fire crackers as fuses. Tee hee. Bigger bang.

Eventually, we ran out of containers to explode, so a period of calm descended. Then someone found another bottle and we decided to mix our special napalm concoction in the bottle with the oxy-acetylene. We carefully placed the bottle – which contained a very small amount – in the bay door of the shop, lit the fuse and all ran like scared mice to the back of the shop.

As the fuse was burning, Dispatch, thinking that the fracas had ended, decided to venture into the shop – through the office door not three feet from our bomb.

We all screamed in unison. "Get back in the office!!!!!!"

Poor thing. We terrified her so bad she crawled under her desk as the next bang went off.

It was spectacular. It lit up the whole street, rattled windows in every nearby building and set off car alarms a couple of blocks up. We were giggling, dancing and congratulating ourselves until police staff sergeant Waldo pulled up.

A veteran of practical jokes himself, he was now forced to don the mantle of responsibility. He got out of his cruiser, walked over to our sniggering mob and gave us a stern look. "Boys, I think things are getting a little out of hand. I saw that last one from the end of the street and we're getting complaints from ten blocks away of gunfire. I know it's you. Now settle down or I'll be back and I won't be so nice."

We all smiled sweetly saying that we would be good little tow truck boys and behave, but could we just finish of the last couple of fire crackers and be done? He chuckled and told us to go ahead, but get it over with soon. He knew what was up. He'd taught a couple of us older guys how to mix the chemicals in the past years after all. Little did he know that we had already prepared one last, much larger concoction.

Waiting long enough for Waldo to leave the area, we walked up the block and set two bottles taped together end-to-end with a fuse in the centre, each one full of our explosive concoction. Everyone hid behind a truck while I lit the fuse. That done, I ran as if the hounds of hell were chasing me. We crouched in anticipation, waiting to see how big a bang we'd created. A few seconds later it started. The flash was blinding, the shock wave knocked us back, and the noise. Oh my Lord, the noise! It sounded like an artillery gun at the Somme.

Shocked gazes passed between us, some guys checking for bleeding ears, but soon we started to smile. Then we started to laugh. After looking around the front of the truck to make sure it had all exploded, we ran to the blast site. To our amazement, we'd left a crater in the asphalt that was about 15 feet across and six inches deep. There were bits of asphalt in the trees nearby, some had hit the building across the street and some lay out in the intersection two blocks away. Car alarms were going off everywhere and the power had gone out in the next block. We stood dumbfounded, looking at what we had done with simple shop supplies and time on our hands.

(Don't try this at home kids. We're professionals.)

The moment we heard the sirens, we knew it was time to scatter. We jumped in our trucks and skedaddled. We passed a number of police cruisers heading to our office with lights flashing and sirens on and there were people out on the street looking around and up at the sky. We decided then and there that our bomb-making days were over for a long time.

The city crew came by a few days later to fill in the crater and repave it. Nobody said a word. Then the following weekend, Staff Sergeant Waldo came by with coffee and donuts.

I thought we were done for and that he was

bringing us our last meal. He called all of us into the garage, while giving us a stern look, and started to tell us about the strange happenings of the weekend previous; how he'd responded several times to sounds of gunfire, explosions and a possible terrorist attack in the vicinity of our office. He told us how the sequence of events, including the subsequent power outage, had kept his entire squad on full alert until shift-end and that the subsequent shifts were told to be on the lookout for bank robbers and terrorists. Our little stunt had shaken up the five surrounding police forces into high alert for days.

We all stood there with sheepish expressions on our faces while he told us this. We had had no idea what havoc we had unleashed. We knew we were done for.

Then he broke into a huge grin and started laughing. "Boys, my officers have become the tightest crew I've worked with in years. Everybody's been on their A-game, totally on their best police sense. It's been incredible. Thank you. But don't ever, ever do it again!"

⋆

Naturally, towmen don't show their fun side to the public very often, mostly because we're not usually dealing with fun situations out on the road. But just as our good side gets to show through occasionally, every once in a while I get to see the good in my customers, too. So often we're dealing with people in horrible situations, at the end of their ropes, that over time, it's not uncommon for a towman to become jaded. We also deal with assholes, morons, idiots, hecklers, slow-ass old farts and people that should have never gotten their license.

But sometimes, a light shines through. Something will happen that makes it all worthwhile. I always appreciate a tip from a customer or a smile from a young child. But what really makes it worthwhile is when I know I've made a difference for my customer. When it's a single dad with two small kids stranded in the cold on the side of a busy highway, I'm the knight in shining armour, pulling up to save them. When it's pouring rain and the young businesswoman is stuck outside her car holding a briefcase over her head, trying to stay presentable for that big meeting she's late for, I arrive and unlock her car, and my armour shines.

This is what keeps me going in a hard industry that chews employees up and spits them out. Some towmen get hardened and grouchy, just waiting for the paycheque, but there are a lot of us who really do care about our customers. We may look like big ugly thugs, covered in hair and tattoos, greasy and unshaven from days on the road, but at our core is a good soul who just wants to look out for the little guy in trouble. And that sincere thank you or unasked-for tip truly goes a long way in helping us get through. It warms our hearts and makes it easier for us to deal with the next asshole yelling at us and calling us highway robbers and suchlike.

I was at the office just hanging around when a middle-aged couple walked in. Their son had been in a motorcycle accident a couple of days before and they were here to see the motorcycle and take care of the bill as he was still in hospital. I hadn't brought the bike in, but I'd seen it in the yard. It was a mess.

They were still in shock at having nearly lost their son and they told me he was going for more surgery that day. I took them out to the wreckage of the bike in the yard. The mom broke into tears immediately and held onto her husband. He was obviously shaken too and asked if I'd been at the scene. I told him no, I hadn't been. I asked gently how their son was doing and was informed that he had a broken back, torn ligaments, a broken leg and various bumps, cuts and bruises. But he was alive.

"That's the most important part, isn't it?" I said.

They both sighed and agreed.

As they looked over the bike and marveled at how mangled it was, I told them that their son would be okay. I'd broken my back some years previous, had torn ligaments in numerous accidents and had had a serious motorcycle accident when I was young. They were amazed at what had happened to me and that I had almost fully recovered. It seemed to give them hope.

The mom was laughing through her tears. "He keeps asking about his bike. How's my bike? Is it ok? Are you all like that?"

I kind of shrugged. "Yeah, us biker types aren't all that bright."

She smiled and took my hand. "But you turned out okay after your accident, right?"

"For the most part," I said, "but it didn't fix my brain. I still ride my motorcycle as often as I can."

They both started laughing and I could see their tension lessening.

"If he still wants his bike, he'll be just fine. When we give up riding, that's when we lose something in ourselves." I asked them about their insurance, then explained how it worked: since he was fully covered, they didn't have to deal with the bike right now, pay for it or worry about transporting it. The insurance company would deal with it all.

I walked them back to the gate and sent them on their way, wishing their son a speedy recovery. They were so happy and relieved that, after their visit, they sent a thank-you letter to the company about me and congratulated the company on being so caring and helpful during such a stressful time for them.

⊕

I've described the analogy of the towman as a knight to thousands of customers over the years. I tell them I have a few coats of armour in the side trunk of the truck that I change in and out of regularly throughout the day. I wear the Black Knight Armour when I'm snatching a car from an impound lot or for city tickets, when towing a drunk's car away, or when doing a repo. I wear the White Knight Armour when doing accident recovery, insurance towing and garage towing. Other than that, I put on the White Shining Armour only when I'm rescuing a family from a dark side of the road, or getting that door un-locked to get the baby out of the summer heat.

And then there's the last set of armour that, frankly, none of us like to wear. It's the old, bat-tered, rusty coat that holds our unhappy times. Like when we're dealing with a fatal car crash, or explaining to a young single mom that she's lost her car for 3 months because her drunk-ass ex-boyfriend took her car and got caught driving without a license. Or, when we've been yelled at day after day after day about what scumbags we are.

I wear all my suits of armour when needed and I can slip into each role very well, but my favorite is to be the Knight in Shining Armour. It nourishes my soul and gives me strength to keep on doing my job. Each piece of shine is a thank you from an appreciative customer, a grin from a kid who just thinks tow trucks are cool, a wave from a previous customer, a referral from one happy customer to a new one, the knowledge of a job well done. So folks, the shine on my armour is nourished by you. Without my happy custom-ers, I am nothing but a heartless curmudgeon, banging away on machinery. Think of that the next time you have to deal with a tow operator: which coat of armour would you like him to be wearing?

❧

It was late in the shift on Christmas Eve and I was at the office finishing up, waiting for my daughter to arrive from Ontario. The rest of the shift had left early and the night shift hadn't shown up yet, running late as usual. Then the Bat Phone – the police line – rang and I was sent off on a police call.

I was not impressed; I just wanted to meet my daughter and go home for the holidays. Fucking night crew. Always late. Oh well, cops can't wait. Gotta go.

While I was hauling ass towards downtown, with, thankfully, no traffic this time of evening, my kid called and said she'd soon arrive at the office from the airport. I told her to just hang out there until I got back. Now I was really pissed. Never fails: yet another important family time and I was stuck in a truck.

I got to the call, threw on the lights, then walked up to the officer who was standing beside a middle-aged guy sitting on the curb. Poor guy had been crying, obviously having a crappy night, getting pulled over and towed on Christmas eve.

Probably drunk, I figured. The idiot.

The cop handed me the keys to the man's car. "No insurance," he said, "no file number. He's ok to just run him home rather than the yard."

This meant the guy wasn't being charged and the cop was giving him a break by only making him pay the tow fee and not hundreds of dollars in fines along with the hassle of walking home and the car going to the yard.

I asked where home was and the answer was the other end of town.

Great. More time until I see my kid.

I dropped the deck, gruffly told the guy to get in the truck before throwing the car on, strapping quickly and climbing up into the cab. I pulled out and started heading towards buddy's place.

He started talking quietly. "Thank you so much for taking me home, sir. I was just trying to get a Christmas present for my daughter who I get to see for the first time in years tomorrow. I knew I had no insurance, but I found out only an hour ago that I was allowed to see her and I had to get to London Drugs, which is the only place open this time of night. Then I got pulled over and didn't even get there. How much is this tow going to cost me, sir?"

"Ninety bucks plus tax," I replied, thinking I'd give him the base price for a police tow to give him a break.

Tears streamed down his face and he turned to look out the window. "There goes my present," I barely heard him say.

He fell silent for a while, staring blankly out the window. I'm not the most sensitive person in the world, but even I felt for this guy. I could sympathize about missing his kid, since mine was sitting at the office at that very moment and I hadn't seen her in a couple of years. We rode along in silence.

He pointed out the parking lot. "It's down at the end."

I pulled up, jumped out and started unloading. I saw the fella out of the corner of my eye, counting his money and digging for change to make up the difference. With his car now in the parking spot, I handed him the keys.

He offered a wad of crumpled bills and a

handful of change. "It's all there sir. I'm sorry I had to drag you out tonight."

I looked him right in the face, wrapped my hand over his to close his fingers around the money. "Merry Christmas, dude."

He tried to smile. "And you too." He was still offering the money.

Once again, I closed his hand and pushed it gently back towards him. This time, I said more forcefully and with emphasis, "Merry Christmas, dude."

Then he got it. His face cracked with emotion and he pulled me into the biggest bear hug I'd had in a long time. "Thank you sir, you're an angel. Now I can still get my baby a present."

I hug him back and smile, tearing up a bit myself. "Sometimes angels wear fluorescent. We come when needed. Now go get on the bus and get your girl a present. Enjoy your time with her."

Once I got back in the truck, I grabbed the radio and called in.

Dispatch asked for the information and I replied: "That call never happened, okay? I'll be there in twenty."

A little confused, Dispatch gave the all clear and I hastened back to greet my daughter. It made the reunion so much sweeter to see my baby, knowing that I'd helped another man have Christmas with his baby.

The Bad

SOMETIMES TOW TRUCK operators are called on to assist in investigations involving fatalities. As members of the emergency services team, we have to be prepared to use our skills and equipment to help save lives and to clean up after horrific, tragic accidents. Many of us have had years of training and spent countless hours doing courses to further our education. We practice our skills to make sure we offer the best quality service to our customers and spend more than our share of time in the pouring rain, freezing cold and baking sun, working hours of overtime to get the job done.

Often, we store the vehicles during an investigation. Most of the time it's just a mechanical investigation, but sometimes much more is needed. Tow trucks transport suspect vehicles to scales, recreate scenes and even transport suspect vehicles to racetracks for performance testing. Some of my most interesting times have been spent with accident investigators, speculating on the finer points of some particular nuance of an incident.

Unlike the more well-known fire, police and ambulance members, we are not usually in the limelight; we quietly go about our jobs with little or no recognition. We don't have regular post-accident counseling or paid days off to deal with trauma, or even regular time to process our feelings. We live in a male-dominated world with all the sensitivity of:

Just get on with it.
No time for tears.
Buck up.
Feelings are for pussies.

I'm really not sure why this is, but it could be that many of us come from families that still think that way. So many of the guys I've worked with over the years have come from broken families, have suffered severe abuse in the past, from drug and/or alcohol abuse and many are on their second, third or more marriage. Some of my colleagues haven't been able to process the horrific and tragic situations they've witnessed and are still living with those demons in their heads. I, myself, have seen too many catastrophic accidents and I have my own demons that still show up from time to time. After years of therapy and a lot of time, I find that I can finally talk about them. It's cathartic to tell these stories, but I still feel for the families left behind. And I have to warn you: this is not a nice part of the book.

꘎

It was a beautiful, warm summer day. We got the call mid-afternoon and when I arrived I was told by the cops to block the road at the train tracks. I pulled across the road and started traffic control where I could see the fire department and ambulances at the corner where the road drops down the hill. There was a large tree on the corner, hanging over the road.

After an hour or so, the ambulances left. The rider of a motorcycle, I learned, had lost control trying to negotiate the turn and slid across the road, bouncing off one oncoming car and ending up under the front end of another. The rider had been trapped under the car and pinned by his motorcycle. He was severely injured and it had taken a lot of time to stabilize him and lift the car up and off.

Once he was removed and transported to hospital, the police were able to start their investigation. Since the entire area was now taped off, I was allowed to come and assist with the investigation. I helped measure skid marks and identified parts of the bike for the crash team.

Laying around the aforementioned tree were some small parts of the motorcycle. I noticed a small bottle of Armour-All lying amongst the debris, so I motioned to an officer who was taking pictures.

"I think this is relevant," I said. "I think he Armour-Alled his tires and then lost control."

The cop initially dismissed the idea, but I showed him the tread of the motorcycle which was still under the car. Both front and rear tires were slick and shiny. And not just the sides: the tread of the tires also. On a motorcycle, the contact patch of the tread is about the size of a child's pinkie finger and when the motorcycle turns a corner, the contact patch rides up the tire, keeping a tenuous grip on the road through centrifugal force. By coating the tread with Armour-All, the rider had minimized his tires' grip and when he leaned the bike to negotiate the corner there was no friction to hold the bike on track. The police put that in their findings and continued the investigation.

When they were done a few hours later, I lifted the car off the bike and towed all three vehicles back to the identification, or ident, area of our compound. Life went on as the investigation continued. The rider's boot was still stuck in the side of the bike and the cast-off parts were left in a pile with the bike.

Some weeks went by and I was talking to the ident officers as they were revisiting the bike for more measurements. They'd done friction testing on the tires and shown that the coefficient of friction of the Armour-Alled tires was the same as wet grass – even more slippery than wet ice. Unfortunately, due to the rider's zeal in polishing his bike and putting the Armour-All on the tread of his tires, he'd been found the cause of the accident. Tragically, due to the accident, the rider had lost his left foot at the ankle and suffered many other injuries.

꙳

It had been a rough week. Extremely busy: police call after police call. I was just unloading a high-security recovered vehicle stolen earlier that day from an Elections Canada booth. Turns out the thieves didn't care about the three full ballot boxes in the trunk.

"Drop and go!" came Dispatch over the radio. "I got another cop call at the Jubilee and you're the only one close to clear. Bring your paperwork later."

I unhooked quickly, jumped into the truck and roared out of the gate for the other side of town. Traffic seemed unusually thick as I neared the Jubilee hospital and as I neared the parking area there was mass confusion. Police were everywhere, traffic was jammed and people were milling around. I flipped on the beacons and started to push through traffic. One of the officers at the caution tape saw me and waved me in, pointing toward the far side of the lot. I approached the gaggle of cruisers, fire trucks and ambulances, trying to guess what might have happened. Too far from any roofs for a jumper.

I pulled up and walked over to the police. Waldo was there.

"Glad it's you and not a rookie," he said. "It's pretty messy."

He walked me over to a compact car. There was a small hole in the roof and a dark pool on the pavement beneath.

"Old guy shot himself. Wife was in hospital, died this morning. As far as we can tell he came out here and pulled the trigger. Passerby saw him slumped and tried to help. Paramedics pronounced him dead on scene and have got him out, but it's a mess inside the car. We still have to find the bullet and go over the car to confirm suicide."

"So, no touch inside but outside is ok?" I asked.

He nodded and left me to my job. Unfortunately, the car was leaning against the curb and nosed in. Being a front wheel drive meant I had to put dollies under the car, but that wasn't going to happen since it was jammed against the curb. I called Waldo over; asked if he had the keys and could I pop the car into neutral to slide it away to hook up.

He looked at me as if I had two heads. "You want to go in there?"

I just shrugged and nodded. "It's only blood and brain matter. I'm wearing gloves. Only need to touch the keys and gearshift briefly."

"Okay then, if you need to." He walked away shaking his head.

I took a quick look as I stuck my arms in to drop the car in neutral. There was a fine, pink mist throughout, just a small area with any recognizable brain. It was a small caliber wound, no big explosion like in the movies. I shut the door, hooked up and towed the car under escort back to the station for investigation. Then went on with my day.

✆

Many vehicles get abandoned at the tow yard. Sometimes the owner doesn't have the money, sometimes the owner gives up on the car and sometimes there are other circumstances.

We had an older sedan brought in on a 30-day impoundment. No big deal: park it in the back lot with the rest. That was in May. Come June, the owner hadn't called for his car yet. It was getting close to release time, so I went to make sure the car started. It had a funk about it – not real gross, but icky. We were so busy, we forgot about it.

A month later, we found it again, still stuffed in the back corner of the yard. It was now July and very warm. The car had a stink to it and there were flies everywhere. It seemed the worst around the trunk, but we needed the keys to unlock it. Steve, the junior guy, was given the task of going into the car for the keys and I went with him.

He gagged as soon as he opened the door. "No way, man! That's sick!"

I motioned him back into the car, covering my own nose from the stench. He went in, grabbed the keys, vomited on the seat and came back out. I took the keys, beginning to dread what was waiting for me, and left him heaving beside the car. By now three other guys had wandered over. They stood around me as I turned the key in the trunk, waiting in morbid fascination.

As soon as the trunk lid cracked open, the smell hit us like a freight train. As the lid lifted we all staggered back. There, sitting in pools of their own liquid, were 20 or more crabs, slowly decomposing into the floor of the trunk. No wonder nobody came back for the car. It went to the scrapyard that afternoon.

꒰ꔫ꒱

Another time, a car was brought in on an impound for being parked illegally. It sat at the back of the yard for the entire winter, but as summer rolled around it really started to stink. The windows were tinted so dark we couldn't see in. When a foul smelling liquid started oozing from the trunk, we called the cops. They asked us to break into the trunk with an axe. A couple of quick, well-placed shots and the lid popped open to reveal a human body turned black by advanced decomposition.

And the stink. Oh my God, the stink. The smell of death sticks with you. It is unique. It pervades everything. It can't be washed out. No amount of Vaseline or eucalyptus on the mustache masks it. Even now, I can place it in my memory and identify it. I smell it when an animal dies on my property. I smell it when I visit the hospital. I know when it's around, even if it's faint and most other people can't smell it. My sense of smell has faded over the years, but never when it comes to that.

⚙

I was working in the shop when Rob ran in shouting, "Flash up the big truck! Cop call! Guy caught under a cement mixer!"

I ran out and started our medium duty wrecker. Smoke poured out of the stack as I revved the engine to build air pressure. As soon as I had enough to release the brakes, I grabbed the radio. "Ready to roll, where am I going?"

"Hillside and Blanshard," came the answer.

Rob jumped into the passenger seat and I roared out of the yard, engine screaming and gears crashing. Flying through intersections with beacons and air horn blaring, I kept the hammer down trying to keep the truck on the road and not cause another accident. We were asked for an ETA three times in the ten minutes it took to get to the scene.

We slid to a stop and immediately scoped the situation. As soon as I saw the rear of the truck, I grabbed the radio. "We're gonna be here awhile. Keep you posted."

The victim's entire body was under the rear duals of a cement truck and his head had exploded through his motorcycle helmet. His motorcycle was jammed under the nose of the truck. Firemen and police were all around and paramedics were pronouncing death. A huge crowd had gathered. Steve and Jay had also arrived in a smaller wrecker for assistance, but they parked off to the side.

We approached the police and asked how we could assist. They asked us to position our trucks to block the view from passersby and do traffic control. We helped lift tarps and string them to block the view of the horrific scene. Too many of the public were trying to get close and take pictures, ducking under the police tape. A couple of snoops were actually detained because they were impeding the investigation. The coroner arrived within an hour and began her work.

As was the norm at that time, we were allowed to assist in the investigation by observing and noting anything. I was at the front of the truck with Waldo, looking at the motorcycle and trying to find out why the bike stopped in front of the truck. Since the bike was lying on its side, it should've leaked fuel but we couldn't find a puddle or streak. We stood the bike up and I unhooked the fuel line. The tank was empty.

The bike had stalled because it was out of gas!

Unbelievably, the rider had passed the cement

truck as it idled at a red light, unseen by the driver. When he stopped for the light in front of the truck, he'd been invisible in its blind spot ahead. And then, when the light turned green and the huge cement truck started to roll forward, his bike stalled and he went under.

I shivered at the thought. Looking close at the front bumper, I noticed a mark. It was a streak that ran from the top of the bumper, down. It was four finger marks where the rider had grabbed the bumper in a last ditch effort to save himself before he was dragged underneath. I could feel the terror and panic emanating from it. I shivered again and pointed it out to Waldo. He took pictures of the whole area and continued under the truck.

As the coroner continued her investigation, we conferred with the firemen on how to get the body out without further damage. A number of scenarios were discussed, but, finally, it was decided to lift the axle and truck with air bags and slide the body onto a spine board, then remove it.

After about three hours, it was time to remove the body. The air bags were positioned and the lines were run. I took my position at the shoulder. When we had eight inches of clearance and the truck was blocked up, I lifted the rider's shoulders to assist in sliding the spine board under. Once the board was beneath him, we pulled him out and carried him over to a waiting ambulance. Then, the cement truck was lowered to the ground and the investigation continued.

After some argument with the driver and management of the cement company, it was decided that I could move the truck as part of the investigation for CVSE (Commercial Vehicle Safety Enforcement). I went through a complete brake system check and all the other tests, including acceleration and braking right on scene. Then, the truck was taken to be weighed and our job was done. The motorcycle was towed to our secure compound and the four of us drivers went for a sit down.

Rob and I had been to more than our fair share of fatal accident scenes, but Steve and Jay were new at this. We sat and talked for awhile to make sure the two new guys weren't completely traumatized.

Those images have been burned in my mind; those four finger marks scraped across the bumper, a man's last, desperate fight against death.

※

It was around 3:00pm when the call came in.

We knew that a major accident had happened at Cook and Pandora a few hours ago and that there were fatalities. The story was that a couple of street racers had lost control and killed pedestrians.

I arrived in the deck truck and was led under the tape to the grisly scene. There was blood all over the pavement and sidewalk. A concrete garbage can had been catapulted down the sidewalk from near a bus stop on the corner. A black sports car was sitting in the middle of the road, facing oncoming traffic. The blood trail followed it. There were paint marks on all four street corners where the bodies were. A couple of bodies still lay under covers, waiting for collection. A shattered stroller lay on its side between the bus stop and the car. The police were out in force, taking pictures and doing measurements.

I was given the go ahead to load the car and told not to touch anything, but I was handed latex gloves first.

"You'll need these before you load," the officer said, handing them to me. "It's pretty messy under there."

I backed up to the car and dropped my deck. As I bent down to hook up, I could see entrails hanging from the undercarriage. The entire underside of the car was coated with blood, bits of skin, hair and small body parts. I fought down the gag reflex and hooked up. I slid skates under the wheels so it would slide up my deck easily. Once loaded, I was given a police escort directly to the identification garage at the police station.

If I remember correctly, three people died and many more were seriously injured in the crash, which had involved two teens street-racing down Pandora, then trying to take the right hand corner at high speed. One lost control and veered into the crowded bus stop.

A few days later, I was called to pick the car up from the station: the Identification Team was finished with it and now it was time for the Crash Analysis Team to take over. I took the vehicle, again under police escort, to a deserted, secure area for speed testing. The police-designated inspector did a full mechanical inspection, then proceeded to put the car through harder and harder maneuvers. They were measuring yaw and drift at specific speeds with a radar gun to accurately pinpoint the actual speed of the car at the time of impact by comparing to the skid marks from the scene. Although I was never told the final results of the tests, I do know that speeds in excess of 120km per hour were tested.

Only after these tests were done were we allowed to rinse the car's undercarriage of its macabre coating. It was done over gravel to let the blood drain away. The car was returned to our compound and tucked away in the back until the trial.

And we just carried on with our fucking job.

❧

I was woken from a dead sleep by the pager. Pulling clothes on and tumbling into my boots, I called in.

"RCMP on the Hat, MVA," was all the information I was given.

I pulled out and started on my way. A rare danger had descended on the Victoria roads: black ice. Sheer, invisible black ice in a city that panicked at the first sight of frost, and not a salt truck in sight.

I pulled out onto the highway and was cruising at around 80km per hour when I started to slide. One way, then the other. All I could do was ride that heavy steering wheel and dance the pedals to try and keep three tons of truck out of the ditch. Finally regaining control, I backed off the gas. A lot.

While taking Deadman's Corner at the base of

the Malahat, I came across a police cruiser; lights on, parked rather oddly. His rear tires were on top of the K-rail. I pulled over with my beacons on and promptly fell on my ass as I got out of the truck.

The cop skated over. "Can you get me off quick? I've got to get to the scene."

I thought he *was* the accident, but he was just the appetizer. I hooked on, lifted his tail off the rail and followed him up the mountain road.

What I arrived at was a nightmare of mangled metal. A small car had been rear-ended by a large truck, then stuffed under another truck that had been coming the other way. The car had spun clear, ejecting one passenger and a cloud of debris. The firemen had already removed the other two passengers, who'd been evacuated by ambulance, but the driver was still in the car.

There was no rush to get her out. Her head was in the back seat and the rest of her was trapped in the crush, still in the driver's seat, belted in. The roof had been peeled back like a sardine can. Her hands were still on the wheel.

It was quiet all around. There was the sound of trucks and tools, but no talking. Even the little bit necessary was done in subdued tones. The decision was made to take the whole unit back to the yard where she could be extricated away from the public view and TV cameras. Plus, the main highway could be reopened and traffic could move.

I hooked up the car and the firemen helped me tarp it down tight. Since the police had all their measurements, we opened one lane of traffic. Both trucks involved in the accident were road-worthy, but they trucks were pulled into a layby and parked while new drivers were sent up to bring them home.

I was escorted back to the compound where I unloaded. I didn't stay to watch the rest of the show. When I came in the next morning, the car was taped and cordoned off. No one would go near it. After that accident, a centre meridian was put along that section of the highway.

Nearly 15 years later, that scene is still as vivid to me as it was the night it happened. Some things you just can't forget no matter how much you wish you could.

⁂

The injuries we suffer from on the inside are terrible, mostly because the towing world doesn't have any good way of dealing with them. The physical injuries can be just as bad, but they're often visible and can earn a guy some grudging respect. At least for a couple of days.

Out in the environment in all weather conditions, towmen are bound to get hurt. Sunburn, sunstroke, hyperthermia and dehydration are all summer risks. Frostbite, hypothermia, icy falls and dehydration are all winter risks. Add to those back injuries, tendonitis, stress, poor diet, over work and sleep deprivation, and you have a glimpse into the daily risks of a towman.

Now add the general public into that equation. I have had customers run over my legs, pin me against walls and put me into situations where climbing through blackberry bushes are the only to get them way out. And that's just the careless customers. Let's not forget about the mean customers who actually want to cause harm. Black eyes and bruises seem to be the vast majority of my customer-related injuries, but a slipped disk, sprained ankle and broken fingers fall into that category, too.

Then there's the weird stuff: scraping skin off my arm while reaching in to unlock a vehicle. Blisters on my feet from standing in work boots for nineteen hours on asphalt.

The long term injuries haven't escaped me either. High blood pressure, anxiety, depression, gastro-intestinal problems, gall bladder, lung problems... the list goes on. Nearly all can be attributed to the lifestyle of driving long hours, eating in drive-thrus, enduring high stress situations and managing unstable pay cheques.

Add to that a bunch of other guys all doing the same thing and suffering similar ailments and you get a volatile mix. Many of my friends in the industry are now middle-aged or older. All of my young friends have watched our ailments come and go and we've all tried to pass on the wisdom of eating healthy and getting proper rest. But in your twenties you're invincible and the offered advice of prattling old farts doesn't always sink in. I'm sure if I took all the tow truck drivers across North America and compared health to career length, I'm sure I'd find that all or most have health issues.

Every day a towman is hurt on the road, usually through no fault of his own. Inattentive drivers have killed, maimed or injured towmen and their customers for years. I was reading an article in Tow Times about a fellow who was crushed under his truck by a semi. It drove up his deck, knocking the driver under the truck. He suffered broken legs, a punctured lung, shattered ribs, severe muscle and emotional trauma. And he wasn't the only victim: the impact drove the car he was loading through the cab of his truck, killing the customer who had climbed in thinking it was the safest place to be.

This poor fellow nearly lost everything: his home, his livelihood and his business just to pay his medical bills. Insurance did almost nothing for him and less for the customer who was killed. All because some random driver wasn't paying attention for a moment. But this fellow is still trying to get back on his feet. His competitors sold him a truck for a cheap price and helped cover his work while he was in hospital. That last part made me smile: we try our best to look out for each other because we understand that, despite all the dangers, it's a hard life to give up.

The Ugly

GRUMPY PEOPLE are a regular part of a towman's existence. I get that: I'm in a business where we sometimes have to take away a person's most valuable asset.

Tragedy and death inevitably intrude upon our working lives. I hate that, but I get it: emergency response is one of the most vital services towmen provide.

What I don't get so much are the crazies. I'm not just talking about loud-mouths and big-shots: I'm talking about shit like this:

᠁

It was early one morning and we were all having coffee at the office.

Dispatch appeared and nodded at me. "You're up, Buttercup. It's a City-ordered cleanup. Go get the Mercedes from this address and impound it. Do what you gotta do to get it here."

Oooh, excitement. I grabbed my travel mug and wandered out to my truck.

Upon arrival, I saw an old van parked in the driveway behind a Mercedes: a decrepit, old mystery machine well past its use-by date. I backed up to the van, hooked it, pulled it out onto the street and parked it legally up the block. Then,

I backed up to the Mercedes, got out and had a look.

Flat tires, engine half-in, half-out, not bolted in, transmission hanging, parts strewn around. No wonder the City wanted it gone.

I struggled to get it hooked, chained and secured, and then crawled back to the yard, beacons on, while keeping a close eye on my mirrors.

Once that wreck was unloaded, Dispatch asked if Id looked around the property at all, as she'd been informed that there was also a van in the back yard that we needed to pull. I remembered a lot of mud in that backyard, so I suggested that Rob bring his flat deck along with me in case I got stuck.

Since I knew exactly where I was going and Rob didn't, I returned to the house a few minutes ahead of him. By now, it was a little later in the day, around 11:00, and the residents were awake.

I parked on the sidewalk in front of the house as Rob pulled up, against oncoming traffic, onto the sidewalk in front of me, just as this guy comes running out of the house, yelling bloody murder. He slammed his hands against my door.

I rolled down the window and, before I could speak, he started in on me about stealing his Mercedes. I explained that the City had ordered it removed and that we were here to get the van from the back yard.

"FUCK YOU, YOU SON OF A BITCH!!!!" came the reply as he tried to punch me through the window. I opened the door into him with my foot and he backed off, retreating to the house.

I could see Rob cackling in his truck as the radio crackled. "That's gonna hurt," he sniggered. "Are you okay?"

"Yeah, I'm fine, but we might wanna get the cops down here for support. He's not impressed."

"Base copies," interjected the disembodied voice of Dispatch. "Calling the police now, just stand by till they get there."

Minutes later, the front door of the house burst open and buddy appeared again, but this time wearing shin pads, a catcher's mask, chest guard and welding gloves. And waving a machete.

He took one step toward the truck before I jammed into reverse and floored it away from the yard, Rob in the flat deck hauling ass the other way down the street.

"33! 33! 33! Get the fucking cops here now! He's got a machete and he's fucking nuts!" It turns out Dispatch was still on the phone with the police when I came through and the boys in blue heard my distress call in due time.

"Cops are on the way, Code 3," said Dispatch. "Stay outta his reach."

Rob and I stayed back about a hundred feet, our trucks' engines running, ready to move if necessary. In what seemed like seconds, a dozen or so cop cars screeched in, lights and sirens blaring, and officers were swarming the front of the house, guns drawn. After a brief standoff, buddy was subdued, cuffed and placed in the back of a cruiser.

Rob and I gave our statements and were told to continue with our duties of removing the van.

Psycho just threatened you with a machete? Whatever man, get back in there.

I backed in between the houses and promptly got stuck. I revved the truck and my tires spun, spraying mud up the side of both houses. There were a couple of old mattresses beside the house, which Rob and I dragged over to use as traction aids. I backed in again, barely fitting between the two buildings, and started winching the van toward me.

Now keep in mind, this was winter in Victoria: very wet and soggy. The van had been sitting back there for God-knows how long and it fought me like a prize halibut. After about half an hour of dragging it sideways through the lawn, creating huge craters and berms, I finally got it in close enough. By now, I was now totally stuck along with my catch.

Rob parked his truck on the street and ran his line to my truck. I freewheeled my winch to leave the van where it was while Rob pulled my truck out from between the houses. It was so soggy, the mattresses were dragged with me and I started to slide into a house. We stopped and re-hooked on the other side of my truck. Slowly but surely, I emerged from the muck. I then dragged the seized van through the same quagmire that my truck had turned into a decent impression of No-Man's Land at Ypres. At least my dual tracks helped keep it away from the house.

This whole time, machete man had been yelling from inside the police car. When I started to do the final hookup, he started pounding and kicking at the windows. Pepper spray time! Of course, a large crowd had gathered after the arrival of police cars and I'm pretty sure the local media was there too. All in all, it was an interesting morning. I don't think he ever came back for the cars.

><

You might think that a towman's yard would be his castle – a safe place where he could relax and contemplate the lessons of the day. Unfortunately, this isn't always the case.

I was sitting in the office with Steve one day when this older fellow walked in. He wanted to get a few things out of his car that had been towed for impaired driving. Steve took his info and asked if I'd sit at the desk while he took buddy outside. I said sure and sat down. They walked out through the shop and over to the car.

A few minutes later I heard yelling and then, Steve screaming for me. Now Steve was a fit, strong, young man who had no trouble taking care of himself, so I sprinted out to the yard.

Outside, I saw Steve and this small, old guy struggling on top of a car. I weaved through the cars and closed in. I saw that the old guy had a hammer in his hand and his target was Steve.

I jumped onto the trunk and pinned the old guy under me, holding his arm down so Steve could break free. The guy fought hard to get out, but he was only 120lbs or so and my 200lbs laying on top of him kept him stuck to the car. Steve gasped for breath and took the hammer away from the man.

"What the fuck is going on?" That was the best I could come up with at the moment.

Steve responded with a blank stare of confusion. "I dunno. He just grabbed the hammer and turned towards me."

I looked at the old guy, who'd fallen quiet and still. I got off him and offered the hands-in-the-air WTF look. He just stared at the ground. I told Steve to go back inside and watch the office: I'd finish up here. So, Steve tossed the hammer back in the car and went inside.

The old guy went back into the car to collect stuff and grabbed the hammer again. I was on the other side of the car, but he didn't come after me: he just started beating up his own car. I backed away, shaking my head, and let him go at it for a few moments, but as he was quite close to other cars, I decided really quickly that it was time for him to leave.

I walked around the car and he tried to run away, still swinging the hammer to break windows and lights. As he paused to take a second swing at a particularly stubborn headlight, I jumped the hood, knocked him off balance and grabbed the hammer out of his hand. Prying the hammer loose, I pinned his arm up behind him, using the walking restraint. I lifted him up, keeping both of his arms pinned together, and marched him forcefully to the front door. That entire time, no words were spoken: it was weird.

I got him out to the street and told him not to come back until he could bring someone else with him. He left without a word.

Back inside, Steve gave me a questioning look. I just shrugged my shoulders and picked up my magazine. Another day in Paradise.

❧

Since common tools can be turned into deadly weapons in the wrong hands, a towman has to take threats pretty seriously. Especially when he's working by himself in dark, deserted parking lots in the middle of the night.

One time I was patrolling a townhouse complex way out in the burbs, looking for illegally parked cars. It was about 3:00a.m. and dead quiet. This particular complex was quite large, with speed bumps and over two hundred stalls separated by hedges, trees and laneways. To be able to sneak in, check for parking passes, load and get out without being heard or caught took some practice and careful movements.

About three quarters of the way through the lot, I found a prize: a Chrysler LeBaron nosed into a parking stall with no parking pass. It was front wheel drive, so dollies were required. I'd have to move fast.

Quietly, I backed up to the car and engaged PTO, but not in high idle. I just let it rumble quietly. I then dropped the wheel-lift – not quite to ground so it wouldn't scrape – backed up, touched tires and then hooked L-arms. Okay, hooked: at least I'd get a drop charge now. Went for the dollies. Struggled and squeezed the 50-pound wheel units and quietly slid the arms underneath. Grabbed the six-foot steel bar to lever the self-loading dollies up to operating height.

With this set-up, each wheel gets progressively heavier as you lift a car and by the time the last wheel is going up there is about 2000lbs of force against that lever. It's a potential death-trap: guys have spewed teeth, cracked jaws, split skulls and busted shoulders when a bar under pressure let go at the wrong time.

Just as I was struggling to lift the last wheel, bent over using my whole body weight to force the bar down, this guy tapped me on the shoulder and said, "Let go of that bar or I'll shoot you where you stand."

I felt him right against my leg. I was pinned between his car and the one next to it with a hedge in front of me. I had nowhere to go except back through him. I paused, weighing my options, then stepped to the side and let go of the bar.

It rocketed up past my face – so close I could feel the wind – and square into the chest and face of a rather large man.

THWACK!!!!

The bar vibrated in the wheel after releasing its pent-up energy into my potential assailant. It laid him out cold, bruise starting to form around his eyes and up his cheek. He groaned, but I wasn't waiting around to get shot if he did have a gun. I snapped the wheel up, threw my lights on and dragged buddy off to the side.

I got in my truck and drove like hell outta there, pausing once I was out of the complex to call the police and let them know what happened, that they might want to send an officer or four to check on this guy, but that I wasn't sticking around.

Guns, thankfully, are rare where I live, but that doesn't make me feel much safer when I'm on night duty. Young, drunk guys seem to transform into dangerous weapons all on their own.

There's a particular White Spot restaurant that doesn't allow any parking in their lot after closing. This might seem simple, but the patrons of the bar next door and of the Sports arena two blocks up don't get it. They seem to think it's a perfect place to park for free rather than pay the exorbitant rates of the lots nearby. So, on Friday and Saturday nights at closing time, it becomes a free-for-all as tow truck after tow truck pulls in to hook cars. We used to sit at the coffee shop across the street most nights and wait while one or two towmen would drive across the street and call in all the cars parked there.

On this particular night, there were only two vehicles to tow and I had one in my sights. The other truck could be easily hooked and towed, but I needed dollies due to it having its emergency brake on and being a front wheel drive. As I hooked up the L-arms, three guys came running from the bar next door. One chased after the departing tow truck, just catching him at the entrance. The second guy followed to help.

The third guy, the owner of my target, decided he didn't want to pay anything and wanted his car back. I explained that no, that's not how it works. He ran over to my cab, reached in, turned off the truck, pulled out the keys and threw them as hard as he could.

Now that pissed me off. Not only were my truck keys on that ring, but my house keys, car keys and office keys. But he didn't know anything about trucks. Mine was an old Chevy: it didn't *need* keys. The ignition was so worn out that I just reached in and started it back up.

I ran to the back, lifted his car up and strapped it down, then threw chains on it for good measure. I finally turned to look at buddy. "Now you've done it. Go get my keys."

In his drunken genius, he decided that he had a better option: he climbed into his car and locked it. I'd had enough by this point, so I hopped in my truck, put it in low gear and started crawling towards the exit with his rear tires skidding. I called on the radio to everyone to get outside the coffee shop, cuz I was gonna need some help.

I dragged his car, screeching and skidding, across the street and into the parking lot of the coffee shop, to a waiting crowd of fifteen or so towmen. Some tried to open the car to get the guy out and one called the police for assistance.

I was yelling at the guy in the driver's seat and, stupidly, he rolled his window down enough to shove his face out and stick his tongue out at me. I seized the opportunity to reach in and open the car door. He, though, had the presence of mind to grab hold of the steering wheel while he started to kick. He was putting up a good fight, I'll give him that.

I grabbed one arm and tried to pry it off while I punched the other as hard as I could. I was able to wrench his hand off the wheel and pull him out of the car. He still had some fight left and started swinging at me. We ended up in a heap on the ground until a couple of tow guys dragged him off as the police arrived.

The police listened to all of the stories and threw buddy in the back of the paddy wagon. When I explained that my keys were still missing, the officers drove him over to the parking lot of the White Spot. The offender was released from the back of the van and told to go find the keys. Now. He was unwilling at first but then one of the officers told him that, if he didn't, he was going to be handcuffed and forced to sit in the back of the van with me alone for 15 minutes no matter what happened. I was still hopping mad and chomping at the bit. Secretly, I willed him to refuse.

He saw sense and started looking, but it took a half an hour to find them in the grass along the edge of the parking lot. And then he was taken to the drunk tank for the night, charged with assault and a slew of other offences.

When he showed up two days later to collect his car, he was much more subdued. Perhaps it was because his mother and father were with him and obviously *not* impressed about the whole ordeal. I was sporting a nice shiner and a number of unseen bruises, but I didn't let on to my pain.

After he paid for his car, his mom prodded him from behind. "Go on. You aren't leaving until you do."

He then looked at me rather sullenly. "I'm sorry for my behavior. I know you were just doing your job and didn't deserve any of the abuse. If I could do it over I'd just pay the drop fee next time."

I was taken aback, but also a little impressed. "Thank you. Next time don't drink and try to drive. All of this would've been avoided with a sober mind."

He agreed and left, hopefully having learnt a valuable lesson: don't argue with a guy in a tow truck. They always win.

And I've got the scars to prove it.

Loving a Towman

TOWMEN are a strange breed, I will admit. It takes a certain type of person to do this job: free thinking, often stubborn, driven to succeed, willing to do whatever it takes to do a job, analytical yet abstract and able to see many sides of a situation.

But with those qualities, comes a caveat. To succeed in our career, we often have to sacrifice time and energy with our families. Towing, and what I gave to it, destroyed one of my marriages. In fact, when I first met my current partner she told me how much she disliked tow truck drivers and how horrible they were. Two of her uncles had been operators for much of their career (and she thought they were the nice ones) but she knew how they'd changed over the years from the horrors they'd seen.

When she learned of my chosen profession, it cooled her interest somewhat. But six years later, she's still by my side. These days I don't work twenty-four hours a day, seven days a week with a pager on my hip, but when I do cover a shift for our local company, I get 'the look'. She does, on occasion, come out for a ride if it promises to be interesting. I think she tacitly accepts the fact that this is who I am and I'm not likely to change much.

The time I bought an old tow truck from a friend, she allowed it in our yard; when I curse and swear over it, she just smiles and brings me a coffee. I've learnt the valuable lesson that home and family come first and the truck has to take a back seat, so to speak. As much as my wives hated it when I was late or called away from dinner, bed or anything else, deep down they knew that I was going to help someone. It didn't always occur to them in the moment, but, often, their appreciation came later.

Toward the end of my last marriage, the phrase I heard most was: "Can't someone else do it?"

The answer was always: "There is no one else."

That was hard. I was torn between helping a stranded customer and being there for my family. It created resentment, hurt feelings and animosity that crept slowly through the relationship. Even worse, it soured my joy of helping someone.

When we met, I was already towing and my future ex-wife thought it a lark. She joked about how much I worked and found it hard to believe that someone could pull a sixty hour work week and hang out with the same crew in our off-time. We'd hang out with the other towmen and their girlfriends all the time. She'd spend hours in the truck just to be with me.

She told the story of how I sat up straight in bed one night and asked her for the motorcycle straps.

Groggily, she asked, "what for?"

"To tow this damn motorcycle!" I then huffed, rolled over and went back to sleep.

I have no memory of this, but it was spread freely amongst our friends.

As time went on, we got married and had children as did the other guys I worked with: we were all growing up and becoming responsible. A couple who married the same summer as us are still together, but she hates the towing. The difference between her and my ex is what they are willing to put up with and accept as normal.

My ex wanted someone who came home every day with a healthy pay cheque. Unfortunately, being on a commission-based wage system, the more you work, the more you make. The instability of the system made it hard to budget for my family. To have a good pay cheque, I would take every extra job I could get and even work extra days for the extra pay. Priorities weren't in sync between us. I still have those arguments with my current partner, but at least she understands the 'why' of why I do it. Most of the time.

To any man or woman thinking of entering into a relationship with a tow truck operator, be warned. Expect to eat alone often. Expect to have an electronic leash tied to your partner. Expect them to leave in the middle of dinner, breakfast, sex, sleep and any important family function short of birth. Expect to hear about every new model of wrecker deck and its failings, but don't expect the trash to take itself out. Not saying we don't want to, just that we likely won't remember because we're running out the door pulling boots on over pyjama pants to get to the next accident.

Now there are some of us out there saying:

"That's not me, I'm not like that." And that's true in part. There are some companies that work regular eight-hour shifts with no overtime. Their employees get regular home time, benefits and all that jazz. But when shit hits the fan, they're still out in all weather conditions, putting their lives on the line to help someone: standing on the edge of a freeway with traffic flying past only inches away; alone in the worst part of town, going to pick up a repo; standing down a bunch of drunks who don't want to pay for their car; soaked to the skin, frozen to the bone, burnt to a crisp, depending on the season.

And that puts a strain on a family. It's like a police officer's family, or a firefighter's. They know their family member does an important job, but it has inherent risks. Police can be shot, firefighters can be burnt, towmen can be run over or attacked.

It happens often enough. There's a wall of fallen tow truck drivers at the International Towing Museum in Chattanooga. It was dedicated in September 2006 to honor all of the tow truck drivers who have died on the job. The International Towing Museum also sponsors a Survivors' Fund to help the families of fallen towmen.

I joke to customers that, years ago, some punk told me to "go play in traffic" and I've never stopped. I'm as careful as I can be, but if it's my time, it's my time.

Imagine sending your husband, son, wife or daughter off to work one day and they don't come home. It's a terrifying thought, one that most families never have to think about, or, it's so far in the back of their mind, it's irrelevant. To a towman's family, it is a daily thought. It's not necessarily a constant, anxiety-ridden, overwhelming thought, but it's there. Chewing away at you. So, when your towman calls to say he'll be late because he's stuck at a scene, have faith and trust that he wants to be home and safe as much as you want him to be there.

꙳

Two of my children have grown up with me in this industry their entire lives. I know they have mixed feelings on the subject. My 13-year-old son has little to no interest in towing, but he does love cars and wants to become a mechanic. My 10-year-old daughter loves towing, much to the chagrin of her mother.

On the odd occasion, I'm asked to cover a shift when my kids are with me. She's glued to my side, waiting for the pager to go off. I usually take both of them for the ride and the boy seems somewhat interested, but my daughter is right in there hooking up, under supervision of course, and prepping the vehicle for tow. At this point, with enough training, I could probably let her hook up a car with a wrecker or a deck truck by herself. She remembers the small details and understands why things are done. She even asks about driving and backing up, although she has no concept yet on how to actually drive a car. I have no qualms about nurturing her love of towing and will gladly train her when the time comes. Without her mother's knowledge of course.

As for how towing has affected their lives, I can't say it has always been positive. I've missed countless school functions and doctor appointments because I was stuck at a scene, out of town or so busy, I couldn't get away. Yes, I could've put my foot down with the boss and taken time off like other normal parents do, but in this world of high pressure, constant unknowns and unstable jobs, I've chosen, rightly or wrongly, to make sure there was always a paycheque to feed my family.

I'm not here to justify my decisions or to judge anyone else. I'm only trying to provide you with a glimpse into the life of people in my industry. My last marriage broke down because of towing, not just because of my bad attitude. The long hours, midnight call-outs, cancelled plans, late for dinners, irregular income, high stress and heavy workload all took their toll.

I have no doubt it affected my relationship with my children in a negative way. They can rationalize many things, but the deep down emotions will stay with them. I can only hope they remember the positives more than the negatives. I've taken both of them in the truck light parade at Christmas numerous times and I know they've both enjoyed that. I have kept countless of pictures and paintings from their early years of me (stick man) and my truck (or variation of). My daughter still asks if I'm going to take her out in the truck. She even asks me to call my friend I cover for occasionally and asks if we can work for him. As I rebuild the old truck in our yard, both children are with me, learning what's what in the mechanical world.

What I can only hope is that my kids know why I choose to do this job. The stupid hours and horrible working conditions are an unpleasant requirement: they're not why I do it.

The gratification comes from a smile on a customer's face when I show up in the middle of the night to save their sorry ass from freezing on the side of the highway. The satisfaction comes from towing a drunk's car from a roadblock to get one more idiot off the road.

I've had some of the most personal and revealing conversations with complete strangers I've just met on the side of the road. Some have got me thinking about myself and many have been the inspiration for this book. All I can do is try and express my experiences with honesty and maybe some families will better understand.

Life In the Fast Lane

My INTRODUCTION to towing was: "Here's the keys, don't break anything."

I started towing almost by accident. After getting out of college, I took a job at a small, two-bay garage in rural Ontario. We had four gas pumps and a regular clientele. Throughout the year, I worked in the garage as an apprentice mechanic and pumped gas as needed. We had an old, sling-only tow truck that had been around for years, but it rarely got used as it had so many issues and there was a towing company in the next village that we worked well with. But on a certain winter morning, with the mercury near -40 degrees, we needed to get that old beast started to go out to rescue a car in the country.

Usually, on those really cold days either me, the boss or the boss's son would take our own personal 4x4 truck out to do no-starts, since it was usually just a car with a dead battery or flooded engine. But during the coldest times in winter, the other tow companies would be overloaded and – since we were technically a CAA contractor with a tow truck – we did occasionally get called out. This was one of those times.

It was a simple tow back to the shop, but for

a nineteen-year-old kid, it was exciting – a step out into a big new world. I didn't break anything, thus officially complying with my orders, but it was pretty scary making sure I didn't. In those days, steel bumpers were the norm and slings were still commonplace. Wheel-lifts were a brand new invention and only a few towers had them. Flat-decks were so rare, you barely ever saw them unless you went deep into the city.

After my first foray into towing I knew I enjoyed it. Not only was it a break from the monotony of the garage, but I was free and out on my own. Sure, I still had rules to follow, but in a sense, I was my own boss. At least for an hour or so. The responsibility was purely on my shoulders to keep a vehicle safe and secure. Often, I was handed a sheet of paper with a dozen call numbers on it and sent out. No cell phones in those days: there wasn't even a CB radio. If I got stuck or in trouble, I was on my own. There were a few tough situations where I was pretty stumped, but I just kept at it and eventually got the car back to the shop.

It was always a challenge going out in that first truck. The gas tank, which was behind the seat, would hold only four gallons of gas before it started leaking into the cab, so I carried a few jerry cans on the deck as back up. The steering box was so worn that I could turn a full revolution of the wheel before it responded. That kept me alert on the road, let me tell you! The wipers had two speeds: off and I'll work if I feel like it today. At one point, in blinding rain, they decided that today was an off day. I pulled my boot laces out of my boots, tied them to the wiper arms and ran them through the vent windows. Then, I tied the laces together so I could run the wipers with one hand, all while keeping the truck straight on the road and shifting gears. With a car on the back.

It's been said a few times over my career that I'm a little crazy or "just not quite right". I was once asked by my instructor in a Wreckmaster course if I wore a cowboy hat when off duty.

I've always thought that I was perfectly suited to this career. In fact, I've left it numerous times to "get a real job" – as my mother says – but only to return. I firmly believe that we, as towmen, have been given a bad name over the years. Sure, there are crooks and criminals in this industry, but that isn't a true representation of our industry.

Actually, we aren't even technically considered an industry in many parts of society. If I tell people that I drive big rigs across the country, I get respect for my skill. If I tell people that I drive a dump truck and run an excavator, I get respect for my skill. But if I tell people that I drive a tow truck, the response is often; "Oh, are you looking for something better?"

The last time I lost a job in the so-called respectable truck driving field due to cutbacks, my own mother said, "Well, hopefully you'll find something soon so you don't have to go crawling back to driving tow trucks."

Over the years, I've learnt to ignore the slights or misguided thoughts of people. A few people have actually realized how much training and skill

I've acquired over the twenty years I've worked in this industry and they do recognize what it's taken for me to get there. My family has suffered along with me through the ups and downs, long nights, longer days, missed birthdays, missed family dinners, the pager going off during family time, the pager going off during one on one time with my lady, the uncertainty of pay, emotional turmoil of a bad day, underlying emotional scarring of a particularly traumatic event or events, and even through the great camaraderie of a well put together group of employees where things run like clockwork.

I've had one marriage destroyed because of towing and another stretched to its limit. I've missed many important events in my children's lives because I was stuck at some stupid accident or pulling some drunk out of a ditch. It took a bitter breakup and custody challenge for me to finally pull back and reassess. But even as I did, I never let go of my skill, experience and love for the industry.

I'd like to see our industry recognized by the government as a full trade – like plumbers or electricians – with all the regulation, training and certification. I'd like to see hours of service, Labour Standards and fair pay for work performed. I want towmen to have family lives and to watch their children grow up at close range instead of from afar. I want future towmen to be respected as skilled tradesmen, not thought of as some dirty, grimy slime ball who just wants to steal your car.

But it's up to us as towmen to change that image. We need to fight the government; fight the big corporate insurance companies; fight the big corporate car rescue firms, and we need to fight the owners of individual companies. Until drivers refuse to work stupidly long hours for ridiculously low wages, we will continue to be taken advantage of.

Don't get me wrong: I know how business works, so before those of you in management or ownership positions pick up those stones to beat me, let me explain. Drivers also need to take responsibility to help the companies make money. Do your pre-trips and your daily maintenance. Lift the hood of your vehicle every day and check your oil and other fluids. Don't let your vehicle idle for hours while you're in the coffee shop or, worse yet, asleep in it. Shave. Wash regularly and wear deodorant. Just because you get dirty, it doesn't mean you need to look like you just spent the last week in the woods surviving on berries. Smile at your customers. A repeat customer is the best customer.

Treat your truck and the company you work for as if it was yours and your livelihood depended on it. Because it does! If the company loses money, you won't get that raise, the shiny new truck, or the basic tools to do your job. I constantly hear drivers bitching about how they'd do it differently or that they can't get a new set of tires. Yet, their truck has been idling at the gate for the last hour while they bitch. And they've now missed a time call and upset a customer just because they've been standing around complaining. Maybe that particular customer will call back, maybe not. But in the interim, an hour of billable time and fuel has been wasted, not to mention an hour of sowing dissent amongst the other employees, which causes stress for everyone.

So, to you drivers: if you want a new truck, a raise and to be treated like a responsible, respectable tradesperson, start acting like one.

And to the employers: if you want good, reliable, responsible employees, start treating them as professionals and give them the respect they deserve. Pay them accordingly. Give them the time to spend with family. Less hours, more pay. Think outside the box and remember that, without your employees, you make no money.

A staff is what the shepherd leans on when he's tired and run down. The staff holds the shepherd up and supports him in all decisions. If an owner wants to grow and become the best, he needs to foster that mentality in his staff, so they'll support him when times are hard, rather than falling out from under him.

I hope that all of you have enjoyed this little foray into the life and mind of a tow truck driver.

C'ya in the Ditch.

Aidan Coles
Wreckmaster # 050479
February 2013